SINGING LOVE

COLIN GIBSON is Donald Collie Professor of English at the University of Otago, Dunedin, New Zealand, and organist and choirmaster of the Mornington Methodist Church. He is married, with three children, one of whom is a professional theatre and film composer. He is a member of the Hymn Society of Great Britain and Ireland, and since 1958 has given lectures and training courses on hymn writing and hymnology, as well as writing, setting and arranging hymns, psalms and other church music. A number of his hymns and songs have been recorded and broadcast on radio and television, published in New Zealand, Australia and Asia, and sung in cities as far apart as Auckland, Vienna, London and Nairobi. They are to be found in such books as *Songs for Worship, Songs of Faith, Sing a New Song* (of which he was co-editor), *Songs for the People of God, Sing a Celebration, New Songs of Asian Cities, Servant Songs, With One Voice* (for whose New Zealand Supplement he was words editor), *Sing Alleluia, Festive Praise,* and *New Zealand Praise.* This is the first collection of his hymns to be published.

Outside the field of hymnology, he has published a number of scholarly essays and articles, and has edited the plays of Shakespeare, Massinger and Ford and a volume of essays on the Victorian novel.

JUNE MASLEN, an Associate Member of the Photographic Society of New Zealand is a New Zealander who specialises in monochrome landscape photography. Her photographs have won awards in New Zealand and have attracted favourable attention internationally. All the photographs reproduced in *Singing Love* are taken in New Zealand.

ANNE JOHNSON is a member of the Photographic Society of New Zealand, and has exhibited both in New Zealand and overseas. She was awarded the PSNZ's Gold Medal for Photojournalism in 1986.

SINGING LOVE

A COLLECTION OF
NEW HYMNS, SONGS & CAROLS

FOR TODAY'S CHURCH

by
Colin Gibson

To my singing school,
the Choir and Congregation
of the Mornington Methodist Church

The Publishers acknowledge with grateful thanks
the help of the Methodist Church of New Zealand
in publishing this book.

Collins Liturgical Publications
8 Grafton Street, London W1X 3LA

Collins Liturgical New Zealand
PO Box 1, Auckland

Collins Liturgical Australia
PO Box 316, Blackburn, Victoria 3130

ISBN 0 00 599137 4

Typographical design by Colin Reed
Cover photo by Colin Gibson
Typeset by Collyer Graphics
Printed in Hong Kong by
South China Printing Company

Contents

Preface   9

New Hymns, Songs & Carols

1	He came singing love	12
2	In this familiar place	15
3	Where the road runs out	16
4	All we asked you gave and more	18
5	For the gift of laughter	21
6	Song of the wilderness	22
7	Great ring of light	24
8	Psalm 90	26
9	Voices	28
10	My Father's ground	30
11	But I say unto you	32
12	Matthew was a lonely man *(John Gibson)*	34
13	Christ joyful	38
14	Ballad of the fishermen	40
15	If all my youthful strength	42
16	Lord of all love	44
17	A summer carol	46
18	Carol of cold comfort	48
19	When Joseph and Mary were turned from the inn	50
20	The mighty sun	52
21	Christ our joy	54
22	The coming of Christ	56
23	Christ the cornerstone	60
24	Out of such sun and air	62
25	Godpoint	64

NEW SETTINGS FOR MODERN TEXTS

26 Son of the carpenter *(Ivor Sperring)*   68

27 Lord of each soul *(Paul Engle)*   70

28 Now the silence *(Jaroslav Vajda)*   72

29 Start again *(Roland Giese)*   74

30 Father of night *(Bob Dylan)*   76

31 I am the great sun *(Charles Causley)*   78

32 Pentecost *(John Bennett)*   80

33 Jesus thy boundless love
(Paul Gerhardt; trans. John Wesley)   82

34 Eternal Spirit of the living Christ
(Frank von Christenson)   84

35 Prayer of protection *(Isaiah Sully)*   86

36 Young beam of heaven *(Anne Ridler)*   88

37 Unto us a Son is given *(Alice Meynell)*   90

38 A stable lamp is lighted *(Richard Wilbur)*   92

39 Three masts has the thrusting ship
(Charles Causley)   94

40 A New Zealand carol *(Shirley Murray)*   96

41 Carol for a New Zealand child
(Dorothy Neal Ballantyne)   98

42 Children's Christmas hymn *(Helen Clyde)*   100

43 The first night *(Eileen Duggan)*   102

44 Carol *(Shirley Murray)*   104

45 I read your signature *(Charles Brasch)*   106

46 A song of Abraham   110

47 A song of David   112

48 The four evangelists   114

49 Seek and you shall find   116

50 Sing, sing, and what shall we sing?   118

51 The helper *(Roland Giese)*   120

52 Psalm 151   123

53 Father forgive *(Roland Giese)*   126

54 How much am I worth?   128

55 Caring   132

56 I've never seen an elephant   134

57 Put me down for a victory crown   138

Acknowledgements   141

Alphabetical index of hymns   142

Preface

Any Methodist hymnwriter whose first collection of hymns and songs is published in the year of the celebrations marking the 250th anniversary of the conversion of John and Charles Wesley must have a humbling sense of the towering achievement of those two great hymnists. Set beside the six and a half thousand or so hymns written by Charles, many of them of ten or more verses and several of them among the finest of all English hymns, a modern gathering of less than a hundred hymns and religious songs makes no more than a very small complement to the monumental work of those founding fathers of Methodist song.

However, the intentions behind the writing of the songs in this book are much like those that animated the Wesleys. In something like the words of John Wesley's preface to his famous 1779 collection of hymns, *Singing Love* is offered as a means of raising or quickening the spirit of devotion, of confirming faith, of enlivening hope, and of kindling or increasing love to God and one's fellow human beings. And if there is laughter and sadness here, doubt and certainty, loneliness as well as an assurance of community, and celebration as well as solemnity, that is because these hymns mirror some of the contemporary realities of the life of faith among the ordinary community from which they sprang. It is my hope that other singers in other places will find that they reflect and express something of their own Christian experience, too.

Apart from the general debt indicated in the dedication of this book to a choir and congregation alive to the Methodist tradition of music as a crucial element in worship, education and community celebration, and willing to explore with me the new and unknown, there are other acknowledgements to be made, for no hymnwriter works alone and the production of any hymnbook or collection of hymns is the result of many talented people's work.

Andrew Johnston, Evan Lewis and Timothy Langley stimulated and encouraged the writing and singing of these hymns. The prompting of Alan Woodley, then General Secretary of the Methodist Church of New Zealand, together with generous financial support from the Prince Albert College Trust made their publication possible. June Maslen and Anne Johnson offered a rich range of photographic images to match and complement the words of the hymns. Clive Arlidge gave expert advice on the selection of Maori design elements. Sally Ferard of Collins Liturgical Publications and Deirdre Parr of Collins Liturgical New Zealand, assisted and advised at every stage of the production of the book.

And now, here are songs for the singing; songs for singing love.

Colin Gibson
February 1988

New Hymns, Songs & Carols

◈ 1 ◈
He came singing love

SINGING LOVE
♩ = 96
UNISON

1 He came sing-ing *love* and he lived sing-ing *love;* he

died, _____ sing-ing *love.* He a-rose _____ in

si - lence. For the *love* to go on we must

make it our song; you and I _____ be the sing- ers. _____

1 He came singing love and he lived singing love;
   he died, singing love.
   He arose in silence.
   For the love to go on
   we must make it our song;
   you and I be the singers.

2 He came singing faith and he lived singing faith;
   he died, singing faith.
   He arose in silence.
   For the faith to go on
   we must make it our song;
   you and I be the singers.

3 He came singing hope and he lived singing hope;
   he died, singing hope.
   He arose in silence.
   For the hope to go on
   we must make it our song;
   you and I be the singers.

4 He came singing peace and he lived singing peace;
   he died, singing peace.
   He arose in silence.
   For the peace to go on
   we must make it our song;
   you and I be the singers.

◈ 2 ◈
In this familiar place

for the Freeland Chapel

2 In halting song and word
   the music of your voice is heard.

3 Among these friends of mine
   I taste the company divine.

4 Within this narrow sphere
   I learn that you are everywhere.

◈ 3 ◈
Where the road runs out

COLUMBUS

♩ = 116

UNISON

1 Where the road runs out and the sign - posts end, where we

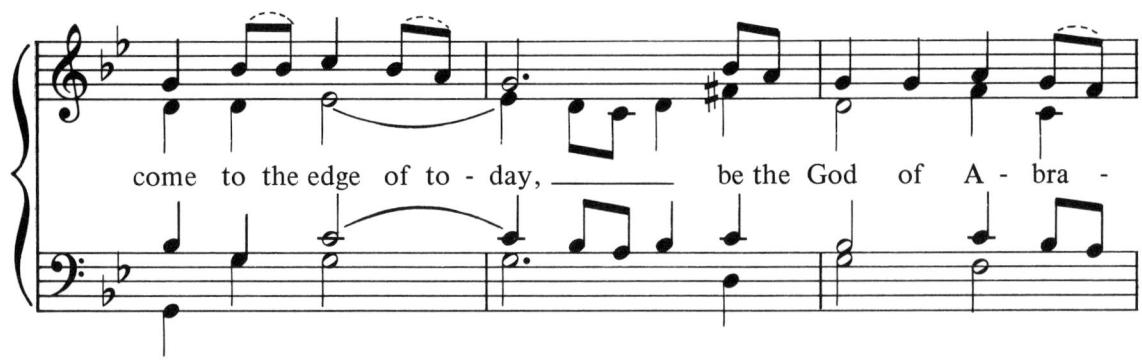

come to the edge of to - day, _____ be the God of A - bra -

ham for us; send us out up - on our_ way. *Lord,_*

Refrain

you were our be - gin - ning, the_ faith that gave_ us_ birth. We_

look to you, our end - ing, our_ hope for heaven and_ earth.

1 Where the road runs out and the signposts end,
   where we come to the edge of today,
   be the God of Abraham for us;
   send us out upon our way.
   Lord, you were our beginning,
   the faith that gave us birth.
   We look to you, our ending,
   our hope for heaven and earth.

2 When the coast is left and we journey on
   to the rim of the sky and the sea,
   be the sailor's friend, be the dolphin Christ;
   lead us on to eternity.

3 When the clouds are low and the wind is strong,
   when tomorrow's storm draws near,
   be the spirit bird hovering overhead
   who will take away our fear.

◇ **4** ◇

All we asked you gave and more

500 MILES

American folk melody

♩ = 72

1 All we asked you gave and more, then you open-ed ev-ery

door, and you blessed us with the free-dom that we

Refrain

craved. _____ The love of God is ve-ry

great, the love of God is ve-ry deep, the love of

God is nev-er end-ing, come what may.

1 All we asked you gave and more,
  then you opened every door,
  and you blessed us with the freedom that we craved.
  The love of God is very great,
  the love of God is very deep,
  the love of God is never-ending,
  come what may.

2 Lord, we left you far behind,
  tried to drive you from our mind,
  spent our life in living high and recklessly.

3 Now our very souls are worn,
  we are restless and forlorn,
  and we know this isn't how it ought to be.

4 Not a penny to our name,
  only hunger, only shame;
  may we dare to call you Father once again?

5 Will you meet us on the way
  as we journey toward the day
  when the dead return to life, the lost are found?

◈ 5 ◈
For the gift of laughter

for Mabel Chandler

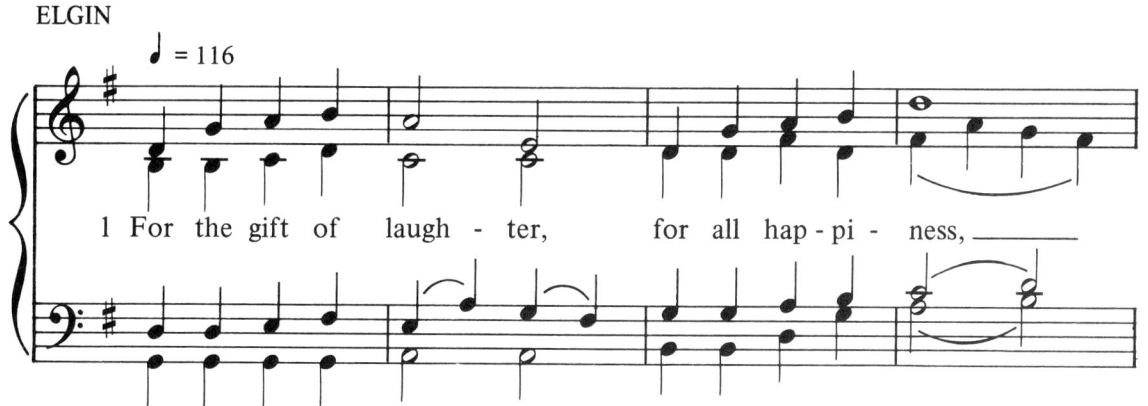

1 For the gift of laugh - ter, for all hap - pi - ness,

for the cheer - ful spi - rit, Lord of joy, we bless.

2 For the heart's devotion,
for all prayerfulness,
for each act of worship,
Lord of souls, we bless.

3 For the deeds of service,
for all thoughtfulness,
for a life poured out,
O servant Lord, we bless.

4 For a love unstinted,
for all tenderness,
for the gift of friendship,
Loving Lord, we bless.

◈ 6 ◈

Song of the wilderness

for Marion Kitchingman

GLENROSS

1 When we go in - to the night, leave be - hind each friend-ly

light, when the sha - dows of the world have gath-ered round, ____

__ may we know there is no place se - par - a - ted from your

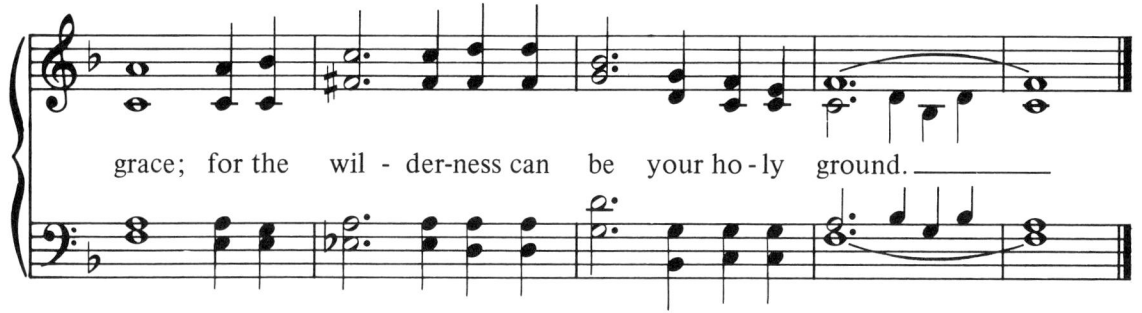

grace; for the wil-der-ness can be your ho-ly ground. _____

1 When we go into the night,
 leave behind each friendly light,
 when the shadows of the world have gathered round,
 may we know there is no place
 separated from your grace;
 for the wilderness can be your holy ground.

2 You have walked the desert sand,
 crossed the dry and thirsty land;
 cloud of fire, to bless and guard, ahead you go.
 When we're weak, for us be strong,
 when we're silent, sing our song;
 lead us, God, through every wilderness we know.

3 Forty days you watched alone
 in a world of rock and stone,
 while the voices of temptation filled the air.
 Be the friend we cannot find,
 be the guardian of our mind,
 by our side, O desert Christ, stand ever there.

4 On your name, O Lord, we call,
 mighty saviour of us all,
 hold us safe within the compass of your love.
 Christ who walked the desert ways,
 be companion to our days;
 grant us peace, O Holy Spirit, heavenly dove.

◈ **7** ◈
Great ring of light

HALLEY

♩ = 126

1 Great ring of light, true cir - cle with no end - ing;

clear beam so bright, whose pur - pose knows no bend - ing;

(v.3)

O Word of God, in dark - ness al - ways shi - ning

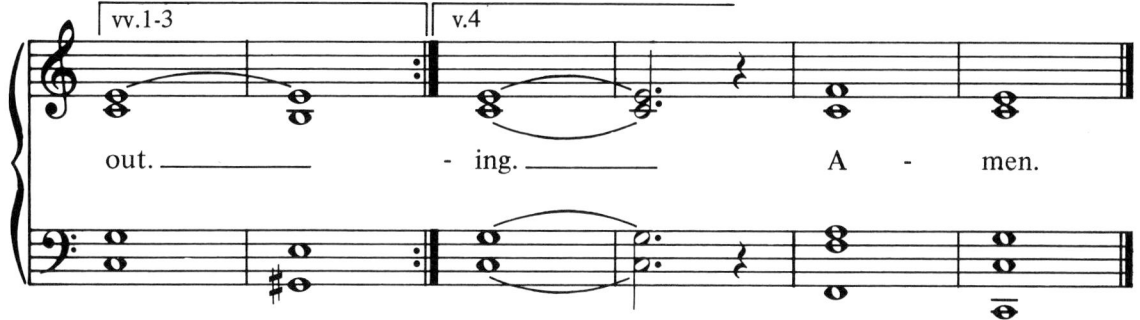

out. ————————— - ing. ————————— A - men.

1 Great ring of light,
   true circle, with no ending;
   clear beam so bright,
   whose purpose knows no bending;
   O Word of God,
   in darkness always shining out.

2 A man who cried,
   upon a cross at Calvary;
   for him who died
   an empty tomb, a mystery;
   O risen Christ,
   all pain and loss transcending.

3 Immortal fire
   of love for ever yearning;
   flame of desire
   for our salvation burning;
   Spirit divine,
   our friend, and present comforter.

4 The light shines still,
   the eternal Word has spoken;
   on Calvary's hill
   the power of death is broken;
   and I receive
   the life, the joy, the loving. Amen.

8

Psalm 90

for Margaret Wood

ARBOR

1 Lord, you have been our dwell-ing place in ev-'ry time and age; be-fore the moun-tain peaks were born, be-fore the world was made, from ev-er-last-ing you are God, to end-less years the same, but we are called back to the earth, the dust from which we came.

1 Lord, you have been our dwelling place
  in every time and age;
  before the mountain peaks were born,
  before the world was made,
  from everlasting you are God,
  to endless years the same,
  but we are called back to the earth,
  the dust from which we came.

2 Thousands of years, before your eyes,
  are like a day that's done;
  an hour of watching in the night,
  and then for ever gone.
  We pass like dreams at break of day;
  we rise with morning light,
  then like the grass we fall away,
  lie withered by the night.

3 Our days are ended by your wrath
  and silenced at your frown;
  our sins lie open to your sight,
  our every secret known.
  Beneath the shadow of that wrath
  life passes like a sigh;
  in sorrow and in labour, Lord,
  our hurrying years go by.

4 We are so soon forgotten, Lord,
  so swiftly pass away.
  Who truly knows your fury's strength,
  the power of your rage?
  Then teach us, Lord, to count our days
  and wisdom so to gain;
  have pity on your servants, Lord,
  so long as life remains.

5 O dawn upon us with your love,
  with gladness fill our lives;
  for days of sorrow send us joy,
  and on our children shine.
  Now may the beauty of the Lord
  be set on everyone;
  O God, establish what we do,
  confirm what we have done. Amen.

9
Voices

for Donald Phillipps

LYNWOOD ♩ = 104

We sing your praise in ___ oth - ers' words; O

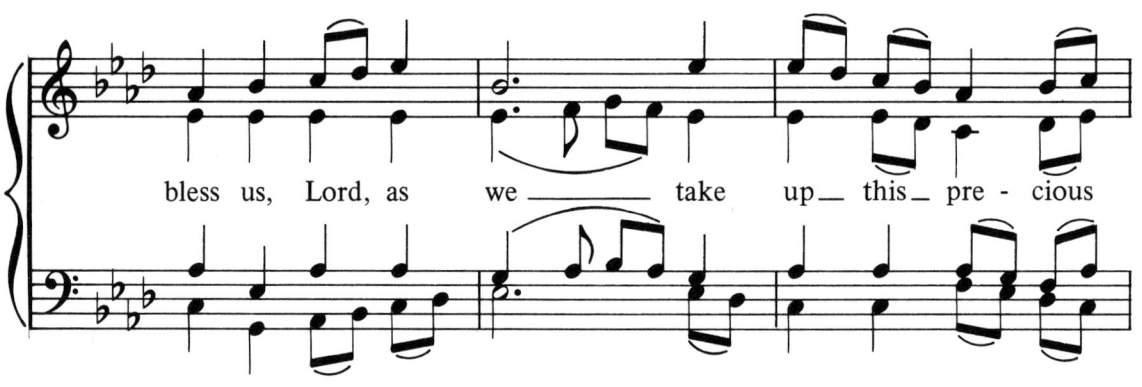

bless us, Lord, as we ___ take up ___ this pre - cious

her - i - tage of faith ___ and ___ his - to - ry.

1 We sing your praise in others' words;
   O bless us, Lord, as we
   take up this precious heritage
   of faith and history.

2 We celebrate in others' songs
   your final victory;
   may all our many voices make
   triumphant harmony.

3 We worship you in many tongues,
   of strange and different sound,
   that so our Babel world may find
   in you its common ground.

4 We use these gifts, by others given,
   to praise and to rejoice;
   Lord, you will hear what heart intends,
   and know and love each voice.

10

My Father's ground

for Glenda Fletcher

BENHAR

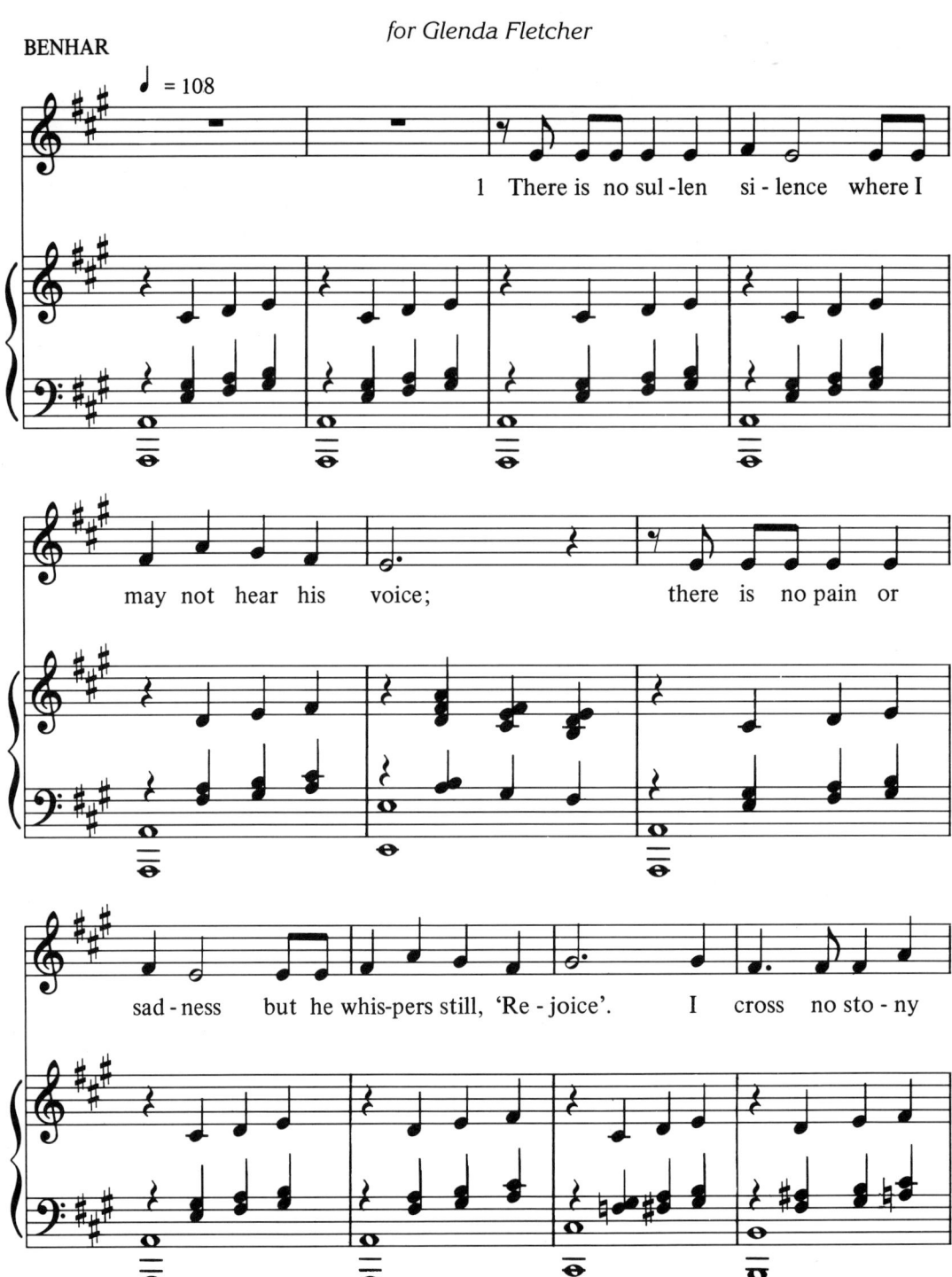

1 There is no sul-len si-lence where I may not hear his voice; there is no pain or sad-ness but he whis-pers still, 'Re-joice'. I cross no sto-ny

des - ert where the lost may not be found; I

walk no emp-ty val - ley which is not my Fa-ther's ground.

2 There is no separation
   which his love may not unite;
   there is no future darkness
   which his truth can not make bright.
   I trace no lonely pathway
   where a friend may not be found;
   I face no desolation
   which is not my Father's ground.

3 There is no bitter struggle
   where his peace will not prevail;
   there is no power of evil
   which, against him, will not fail.
   I lift no heavy burden
   whose relief may not be found;
   I climb no endless mountain
   which is not my Father's ground.

But I say unto you

BROAD STREET

♩. = 69

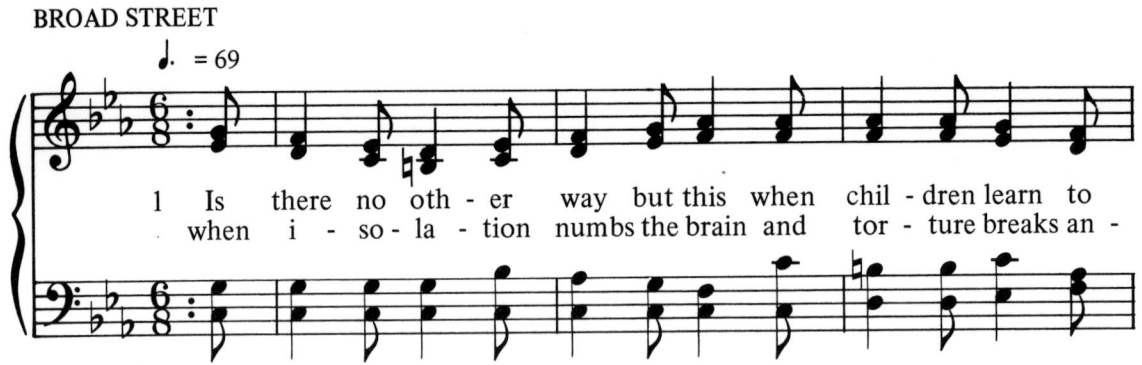

1 Is there no oth - er way but this when chil - dren learn to
when i - so - la - tion numbs the brain and tor - ture breaks an -

curse and kill, Is there no oth - er way but this from
oth - er's will?

ty - rant fear our - selves to save, but eye for eye, and

death for death, till earth be-comes our com-mon grave?

1 Is there no other way but this
when children learn to curse and kill,
when isolation numbs the brain
and torture breaks another's will?
Is there no other way but this
from tyrant fear ourselves to save,
but eye for eye, and death for death,
till earth becomes our common grave?

2 Is there no other way but this
when drug and truncheon, tank and gun
impose belief, or seek to force
their iron rule on everyone?
Must we take up the stone, the knife,
and at the last the winter bomb;
protect our own by taking life,
pit all our strength against the strong?

3 Is there no other way but this,
no other choice before our race;
must hate for ever mask from me
a brother or a sister's face?
I choose another way than this.
I choose to turn from final loss;
choose good for bad, choose love, not hate.
Lift up, my soul, the Saviour's cross.

◇ 12 ◇

Matthew was a lonely man

LONELY MAN

John Gibson

1 Mat - thew was a lone - ly man_ (come, brother, stand by me);_

lone - ly Mat - thew found a friend

(come, Je - sus, stand_ by me). __

An - oth - er sul - len mon - ey day, __ a rub-ber stamp, an emp - ty tray, __ un - less we fol - low when you say __ 'come, bro-ther, stand by me.' __

Verses overleaf

1 Matthew was a lonely man
(come, brother, stand by me);
lonely Matthew found a friend
(come, Jesus, stand by me).
Another sullen money day,
a rubber stamp, an empty tray,
unless we follow when you say
'come, brother, stand by me.'

2 Thomas was a doubting man
(come, brother, stand by me).
doubting Thomas found a friend
(come, Jesus, stand by me).
Within a silent room we stand,
or walk a dry and thirsty land,
unless we touch your wounded hand;
come, Jesus, stand by me.

3 Martha was a worried soul
(come, sister, stand by me);
worried Martha found a friend
(come, Jesus, stand by me).
A thousand clocks, a weary arm,
each whirring moment cries alarm,
unless we find our inner calm;
come, Lord, and set us free.

4 Peter was a frightened man
(come, brother, stand by me);
frightened Peter found a friend
(come, Jesus, stand by me).
And all the angry eyes look on,
the true turns false, the right goes wrong,
unless we hear your triumph song;
come, Jesus, stand by me.

13
Christ joyful

for John Webster

RED NOSES

♩ = 126

We lack the gift of laugh-ter; Faith sits all pale and glum, Hope doz-es on a raf - ter, and Love is strick-en dumb. *Come, Christ, in - to our drab-ness, tell us that match-less jest of life and re-sur - rec - tion, of life and re-sur -*

Refrain

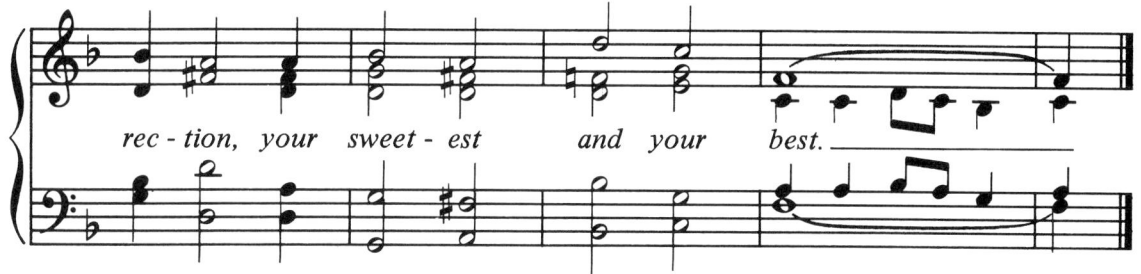

rec - tion, your sweet - est and your best.

1 We lack the gift of laughter;
   Faith sits all pale and glum,
   Hope dozes on a rafter,
   and Love is stricken dumb.
       Come, Christ, into our drabness,
       tell us that matchless jest
       of life and resurrection,
       your sweetest and your best.

2 We know the trick of tumbling,
   red nose and redder face;
   by virtue of our bumbling
   ours is the jester's case.
       Come, Christ, come clown immortal,
       teach us that matchless jest
       of life and resurrection,
       your sweetest and your best.

3 You joined our sad profession,
   made good our foolishness,
   brought clowning into fashion,
   put on our joker's dress.
       Come, Christ, come holy laughter,
       to share that matchless jest
       of life and resurrection,
       your sweetest and your best.

4 Upon a foolish cross, Lord,
   you hung to make us mirth;
   but there you conquered loss, Lord,
   old death became new birth.
       Come, everlasting joy; Christ,
       confirm that matchless jest
       of life and resurrection,
       your sweetest and your best.

14

Ballad of the fishermen

CAROLINE

for Alan Hughes

♩ = 96

UNISON

1 O fish - er - man, come row your boat, come row me a -
way;___ my cap - tain is wait - ing out there on the
bay. His ship will be sail - ing up - on the next tide, and
I ___ will go ___ with him, to stand by his side.

1   O fisherman, come row your boat,
    come row me away;
    my captain is waiting
    out there on the bay.
    His ship will be sailing
    upon the next tide,
    and I will go with him,
    to stand by his side.

2   O fisherman, come row your boat,
    put off from the shore;
    out there lies my calling,
    I'll tarry no more.
    Our course will be set
    for the rim of the sky,
    where surge the deep waters,
    and sea birds soar high.

3   O fisherman, come row your boat;
    my friends good and true
    wait for me to join them,
    old sailors, like you.
    There's Andrew and Peter,
    young John and nine more,
    who've tested the tempest
    and learned the sea-lore.

4   O fisherman, come row your boat,
    there's welcome for you
    aboard the fair Trinity
    with Christ and his crew.
    We sail for the Kingdom
    of Heaven, and, friend,
    his company's that haven,
    his world without end.

◈ 15 ◈
If all my youthful strength

for Clarice Fyfe

ROSEBERY

♩ = 116

1 If all my youth - ful strength I could re

new, and mount on ea - gle wings, O Lord my God, to

you,___ then I would fly___ this rest - less world to

find with - in your pres - ence, Lord, true peace of

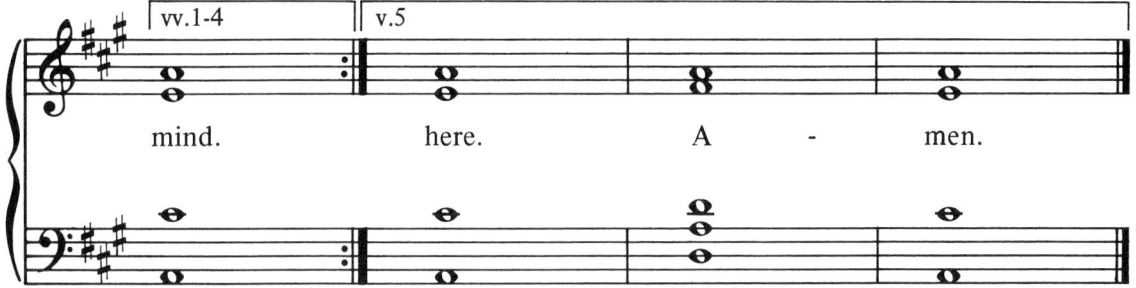

mind.   here.   A - men.

1   If all my youthful strength I could renew,
     and mount on eagle wings, O Lord my God, to you,
     then I would fly this restless world to find
     within your presence, Lord, true peace of mind.

2   But if those heights of heaven I cannot climb,
     and must pursue you through this world of space and time,
     then I will run towards that distant ground
     where Eden stands restored, and you are found.

3   And if I falter, give me then the grace
     to walk towards you, Lord, with sure and constant pace.
     The road I know, the welcome you extend,
     companion of my journey to its end.

4   And when I can no longer walk the way,
     then I will wait with eagerness that joyful day
     when I may greet you, feel your hand on mine,
     and we will sit and talk, O friend divine.

5   For neither height nor depth, nor time or space
     or failing strength, can separate me from your grace.
     I move towards you, know that you are near,
     and you, my God, abide my coming, here. Amen.

✧ 16 ✧
Lord of all love
a funeral hymn

HARMONY

♩ = 104

1 Lord of all love, all life, and death, giv - er of time and place and breath, hear us, as now we bring our loss in - to the pres - ence of your cross.

1   Lord of all love, all life, and death,
    giver of time and place and breath,
    hear us, as now we bring our loss
    into the presence of your cross.

2   Sing us the songs we cannot sing,
    pardon the praise we cannot bring,
    speak all the words we cannot say,
    pray for us, Lord, we humbly pray.

3   That darkest mystery is here,
    sorrow and pity, anger, fear;
    conquer once more, dear Lord, death's sting,
    faith, trust and consolation bring.

4   Though precious dust return to dust,
    in your good purpose will we trust,
    content to place within your care
    she whom we love and grieve for here.

◈ 17 ◈
A summer carol

ANAURA BAY

1 Get up, get up, no time to yawn, put night and wear - i - ness — a - way; the birds are ca - rol - ling in the dawn, the world be - gins — its Christ - mas Day.

Refrain

Come friend, come stran - ger, here's no dan - ger; fol - low shep-herds and

kings to the man-ger where Christ, the Christ_ is born.___

It is literally true that Christmas Day is first celebrated in New Zealand.

1 Get up, get up, no time to yawn,
  put night and weariness away;
  the birds are carolling in the dawn,
  the world begins its Christmas Day.
    Come friend, come stranger, here's no danger;
    follow shepherds and kings to the manger
    where Christ, the Christ is born.

2 Get up, get up to greet the birth
  that ends the reign of dreary night;
  the breakers tumble in their mirth,
  the summer flowers proclaim delight.

3 Get up, get up, you sleepyhead,
  the sea is glittering in the bay;
  the troubled dreams of night have fled,
  the sky is clear and blue today.

4 Get up, get up, get out of bed,
  shake off the sorrows of the night;
  the golden sun is overhead,
  and all the world is filled with light.

18
Carol of cold comfort

Christ the stran - ger en - ter here. Quick - ly, ___ quick - ly, child of light, be born with - in my ___ heart this night.

1 The wind blew keen, the wind blew cold,
the sheep were huddled in the fold,
when Joseph reached a darkened town
and found no place to lay him down.
    Lord, may I with fire and bread
    relieve such pain, remove such dread,
    and, as freely thus I share,
    may Christ the Stranger enter here.
    Quickly, quickly, child of light,
    be born within my heart this night.

2 The pain was sharp, the shadows hard,
when Mary walked the cattle-yard.
She took dry straw to make her bed;
'Come quickly, quickly, child', she said.

3 The moon shone white, but brighter far
there gleamed a single shivering star
when three kings rode, and rode in fear
that Herod's men were drawing near.

4 The frost lay sparkling on the hill,
and all the sleeping world was still,
while shepherds ran by stony ways
to find the child the angels praised.

◇ 19 ◇
When Joseph and Mary were
turned from the inn

SHELTER

♩. = 76

1 When Jo - seph and Ma - ry were turned from the inn and
came to a cat - tle shed, ____ the an - i - mals watched _ as
they drew near, and this is what some of them said. ____
'They don't be - long,' huffed a bill - y - goat strong, and

stretched him-self out on his bed;___ 'they're much too big,'squealed a

grum-b-ling pig, 'let them find some-where else to be fed.'___

2 When Mary and Joseph were turned from the inn
and stood at the manger door,
the creatures looked up at the weary pair
from nests in the rustling straw.
'Later, not now,' mooed a cross-eyed cow,
and planted her feet on the floor;
'this place is full,' roared a bellowing bull,
'you can see there's no room here for more.'

3 When Mary and Joseph were turned from the inn,
a barn was their bed that night;
the animals crowded around them both,
and blinked in the bright candlelight.
'Here you may sleep,' baaed a motherly sheep,
'your pillow my wool soft and white;'
'I'll keep you warm,' hawed the ass, with a yawn,
'for a shelter is everyone's right.'

4 When Mary and Joseph are turned from the inn,
and look for a room once more,
we watch as they pass to some other stall
or stand in a queue for the poor.
'They don't belong,' so it's 'hurry along';
if charity fails, there's the law.
'Not now,' we say; yes, they will go away
if we shut the indifferent door.

20

The mighty sun

YACRE

1 The migh - ty sun leapt up in the sky,

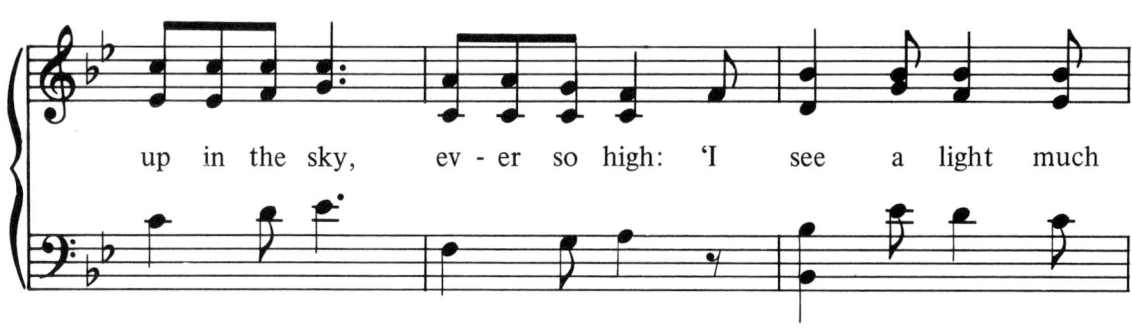

up in the sky, ev - er so high: 'I see a light much

bright - er than I, all on a Christ - mas morn - ing.'

1   The mighty sun leapt up in the sky,
    up in the sky, ever so high:
    'I see a light much brighter than I,
    all on a Christmas morning.'

2   A hawk flew circling, up in the sky,
    up in the sky, ever so high:
    'I see a sign that God is nigh,
    all on a Christmas morning.'

3   A lark went singing up in the sky,
    up in the sky, ever so high:
    'I see a host of angels fly,
    all on a Christmas morning.'

4   A gentle breeze blew over the sky,
    over the sky, ever so high;
    it carried a tiny baby's cry,
    all on a Christmas morning.

◇ 21 ◇
Christ our joy

ODE TO JOY

Adapted from Beethoven's Symphony No.9

♩ = 126

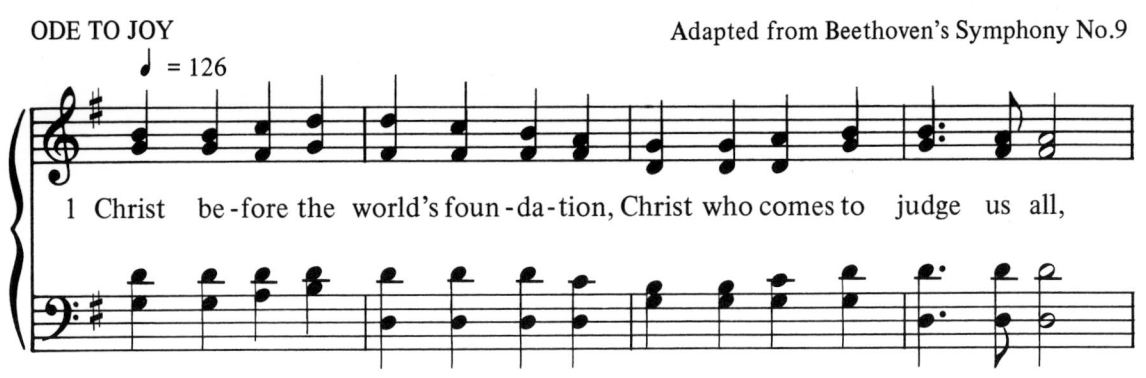

1 Christ be-fore the world's foun-da-tion, Christ who comes to judge us all,

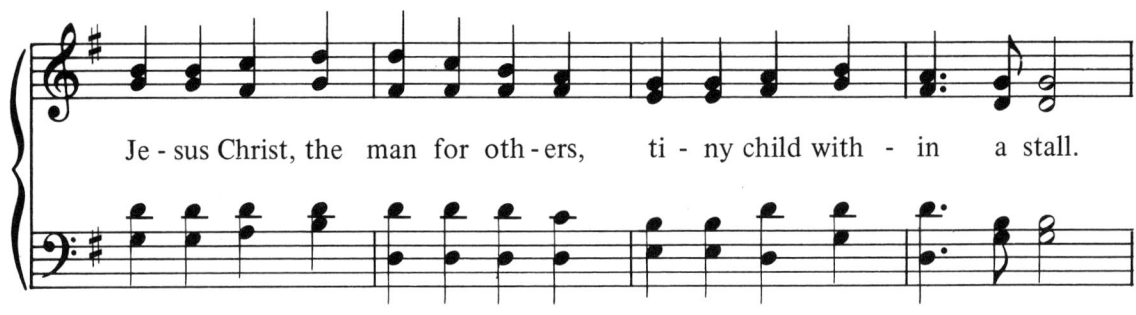

Je-sus Christ, the man for oth-ers, ti-ny child with-in a stall.

We would wor-ship and a-dore you, make an ev-er-last-ing friend,

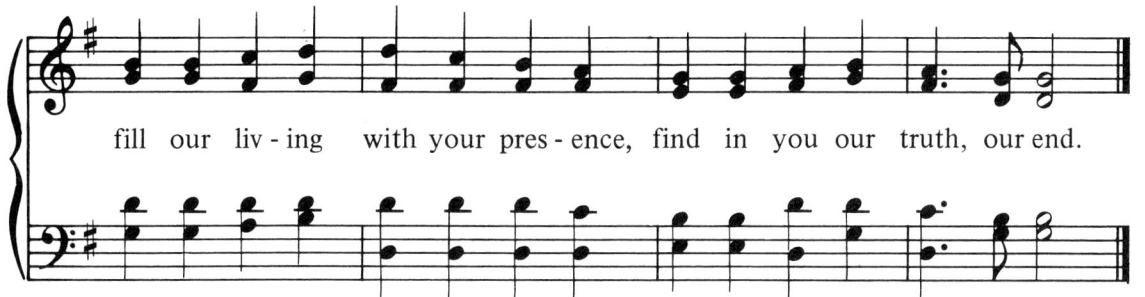

fill our liv-ing with your pres-ence, find in you our truth, our end.

1 Christ before the world's foundation,
Christ who comes to judge us all,
Jesus Christ, the man for others,
tiny child within a stall.
We would worship and adore you,
make an everlasting friend,
fill our living with your presence,
find in you our truth, our end.

2 Take away, O Christ, our trembling,
take away our dark despair,
take our doubts, our hesitation,
change our self-regarding care.
Let us claim your perfect freedom,
send us dancing on your way,
kingdom come, your will be done,
let night be turned to endless day.

3 Christ our joy and Christ our courage,
Christ our resurrected Lord,
Jesus glorious, Christ victorious,
speak in us your living word.
Consecrate us to your service,
grow in Christ till all be one;
strengthen, guide, protect, inspire us,
Father, Holy Spirit, Son.

◈ 22 ◈
The coming of Christ

for Joy King

JOYFULNESS

1 Where we toil, day by day, with no joy-ful-ness,_____ while

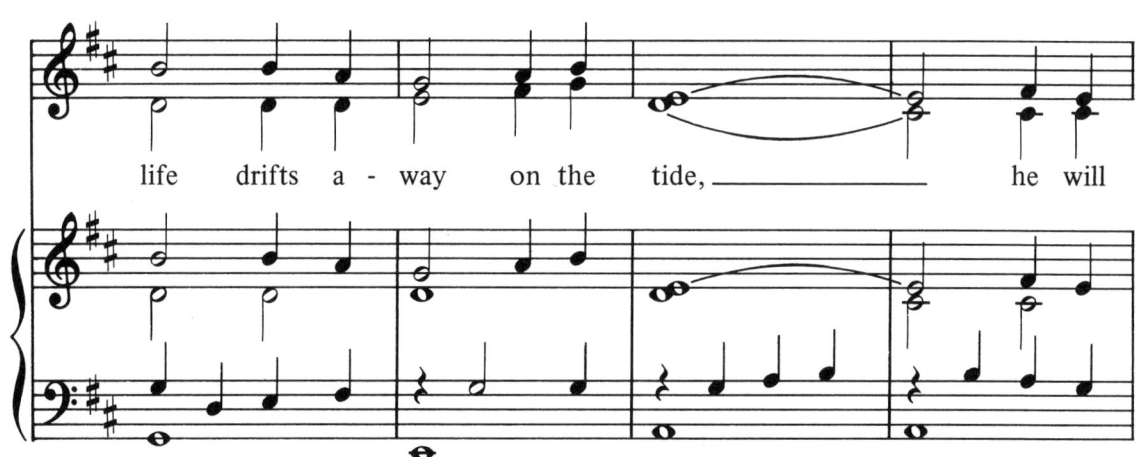

life drifts a - way on the tide,_____ he will

come with his word of de - ci - sion,_____ as he

Refrain

called James and John to his side._____ *This is what he*

sang to them, ___ sang with all his life; this is what he sings to us, ___

Continued overleaf

sings in all his might, I love you, _____ I

love you, _____ I love _____ you. _____

Sustain chord with pedal.

1   Where we toil, day by day, with no joyfulness,
    while life drifts away on the tide,
    he will come with his word of decision,
    as he called James and John to his side.
        This is what he sang to them,
        sang with all his life;
        this is what he sings to us,
        sings in all his might,
        I love you,
        I love you,
        I love you.

2 When we drink from the well of our loneliness,
   and draw up betrayal and strife,
   he will come, as he came to the woman
   who yearned for the water of life.
       This is what he sang to her . . .

3 To the room of the heart's doubt and faithlessness,
   where with Thomas and Peter we stand,
   he will come, be the door shut and bolted,
   with the print of the nails on his hand.
       This is what he sang to them . . .

4 When we weep at the tomb, in our hopelessness,
   for the daughter of dreams who there lies,
   he will come in the midst of our grieving,
   and call to the dead to arise.
       This is what he sang to her . . .

◇ **23** ◇
Christic the cornerstone

a hymn for antiphonal singing

NGAIRE

1 Who will build ___ up - on this match-less cor - ner-stone?

Who will dare ___ to make this mas - sive Christ their own?

CONGREGATION

Peace, and truth, and goal for all are found

on this vast and gra - cious ground.

v.5

A - - - - men.

1   Who will build upon this matchless cornerstone?
    Who will dare to make this massive Christ their own?
      Peace, and truth, and goal for all are found
      on this vast and gracious ground.

2   Who will build upon this flawless cornerstone?
    Who will dare to claim such beauty for their own?
      See the light of God take colour here;
      song and music fill the air.

3   Who will build on this rejected cornerstone?
    Who will dare to take such suffering for their own?
      Lift the cross of Love for all to see;
      show the world his victory.

4   Who will build upon this living cornerstone?
    Who will dare to make this vital Christ their own?
      Grow towards the height and majesty
      of the radiant Son of God. Amen.

❖ 24 ❖
Out of such sun and air

NORTHLAND

1 Out of such sun and air what Christ may come, _____ shin-ing with new and love-ly light _____ on our dim and shroud - ed lives; _____ stir-ring our sleep-i-ness with dreams, vi - sions of life be - yond com - pare. Out of this sun and

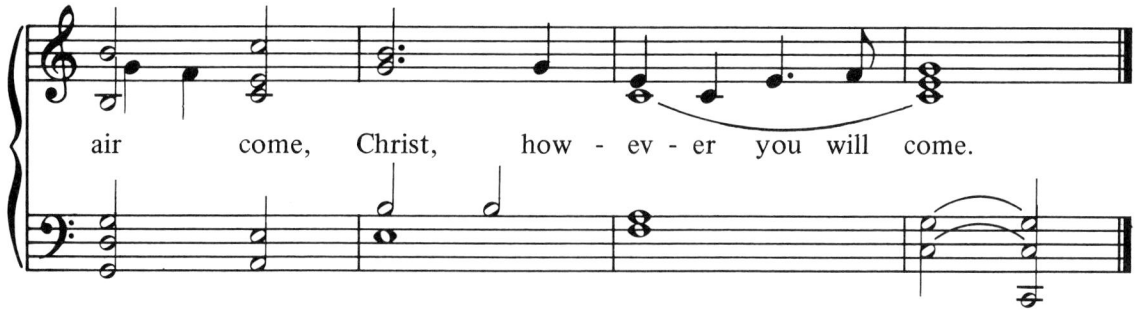

air   come,   Christ,   how - ev - er   you   will   come.

1   Out of such sun and air
what Christ may come,
shining with new and lovely light
on our dim and shrouded lives;
stirring our sleepiness with dreams,
visions of life beyond compare.
Out of this sun and air
come, Christ, however you will come.

2   Out of such cloud and mist
what Christ may come,
blurring the clear and simple lines
of our settled scheme of things;
calling on faith and hope and trust,
daring to danger, trial and risk.
Out of this cloud and mist
come, Christ, however you will come.

3   Out of such sudden storm
what Christ may come,
sweeping across the startled sky
of our calm and peaceful ways;
driving with tempest winds of change,
testing with tumult and reform.
Out of this sudden storm
come, Christ, however you will come.

25

Godpoint

GODPOINT

♩ = 138

Refrain

God is the One_ whom we seek to - ge - ther, God is the Life_ which is

part of us all;_ God is the Truth and the mark of mys-te - ry,

Fine

God is the Love_ and the Joy that makes us whole.

Verses

1 No one_ is a stran - ger, who seeks E - ter - ni - ty;

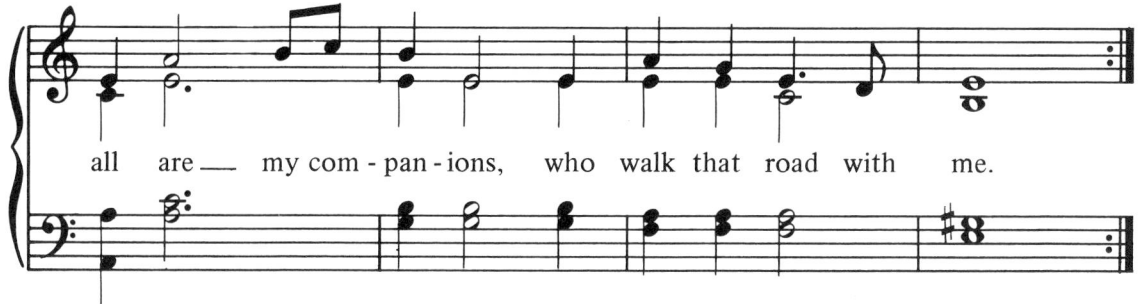

all are — my com-pan-ions, who walk that road with me.

God is the One whom we seek together,
God is the Life which is part of us all;
God is the Truth and the mark of mystery,
God is the Love and the Joy that makes us whole.

1 No one is a stranger, who seeks Eternity;
   all are my companions, who walk that road with me.

2 Freedom is the pathway, for each and all to see;
   you are my companions, who walk the Way with me.

NEW SETTINGS
FOR MODERN TEXTS

◈ 26 ◈
Son of the carpenter

MORRISON

1 To you we come, who made us all, the God of ev - 'ry diff - 'rent

face, and on your name we dare to call to ask for - give - ness for our

Refrain

race. *Where wheels spin and ped-als tread, where smoke and clat - ter fill the*

air, where peo-ple earn their dai-ly bread, son of the car-pen- ter, be there.

1 To you we come, who made us all,
the God of every different face,
and on your name we dare to call
to ask forgiveness for our race.
Where wheels spin and pedals tread,
where smoke and clatter fill the air,
where people earn their daily bread,
son of the carpenter, be there.

2 You made us all of equal worth,
you called us by a common name;
with enmity we filled the earth,
and now divisions cry our shame.

3 Forgive the barriers that we make,
the differences our minds create,
the confidences that we break;
forgive us now for all our hate.

Ivor Sperring

27

Lord of each soul

SOUL SONG

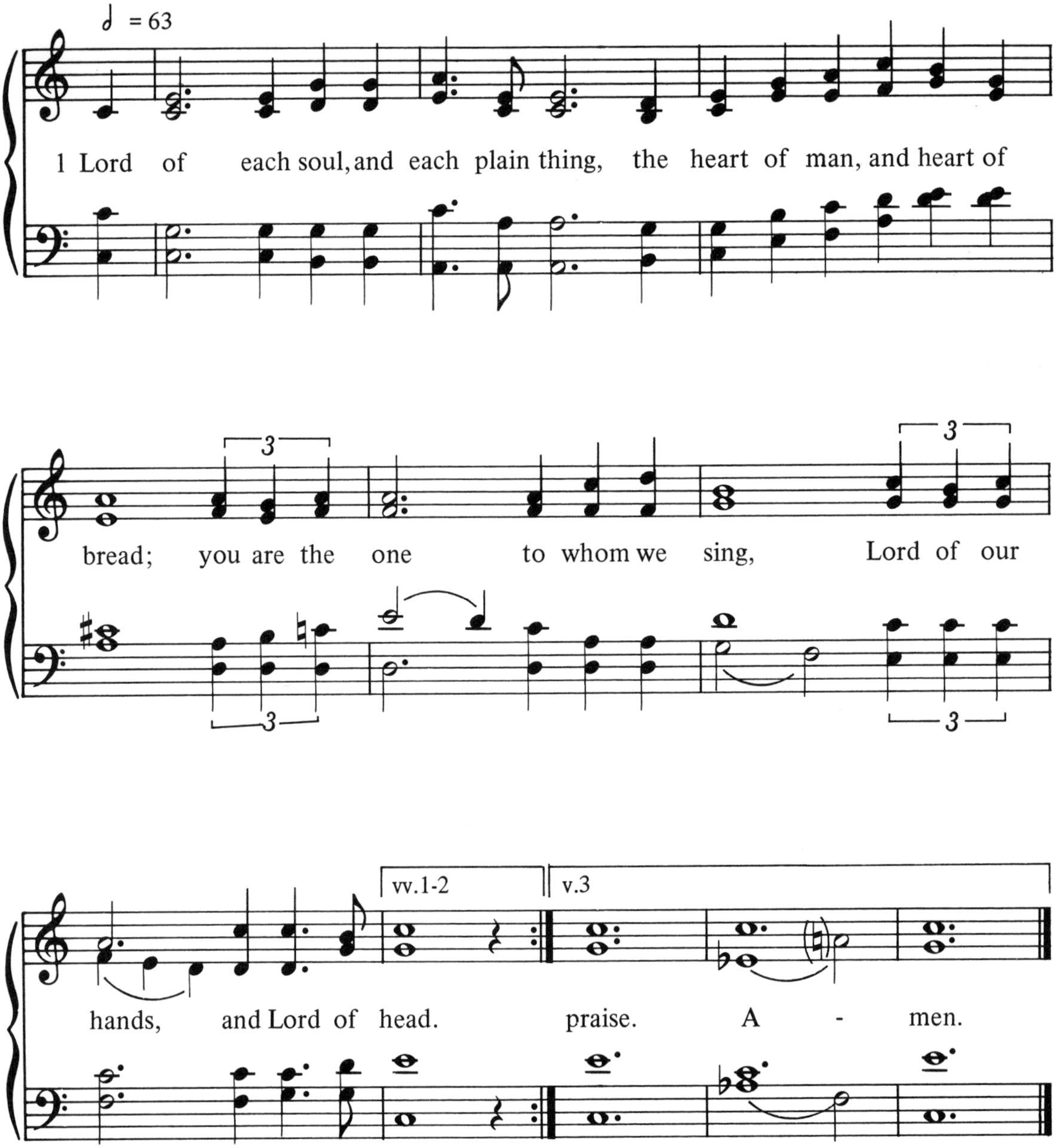

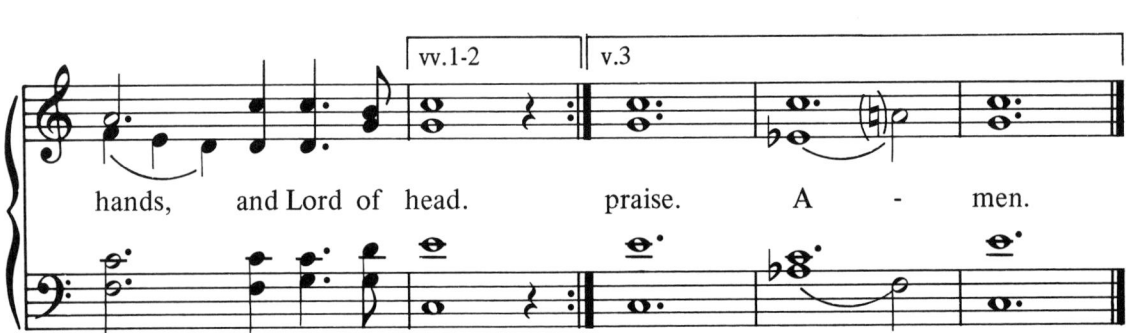

= 63
1 Lord of each soul, and each plain thing, the heart of man, and heart of
bread; you are the one to whom we sing, Lord of our
hands, and Lord of head.
vv.1-2
v.3
praise. A - men.
3

1 Lord of each soul, and each plain thing,
   the heart of man, and heart of bread;
   you are the one to whom we sing,
   Lord of our hands, and Lord of head.

2 Great galaxies of heaven drift
   like clouds of dust before your eyes.
   Here, with our human voice, we praise,
   lifting our little, living cries.

3 From you we take our life and death,
   delight and dread for all our days.
   Whether with proud or painful breath,
   still we will thank you, still give praise. Amen.

Paul Engle (altered)

28
Now the silence

for John Gerry

GALLOWAY

1 Now the si - lence, now the peace, now the emp - ty hands up -

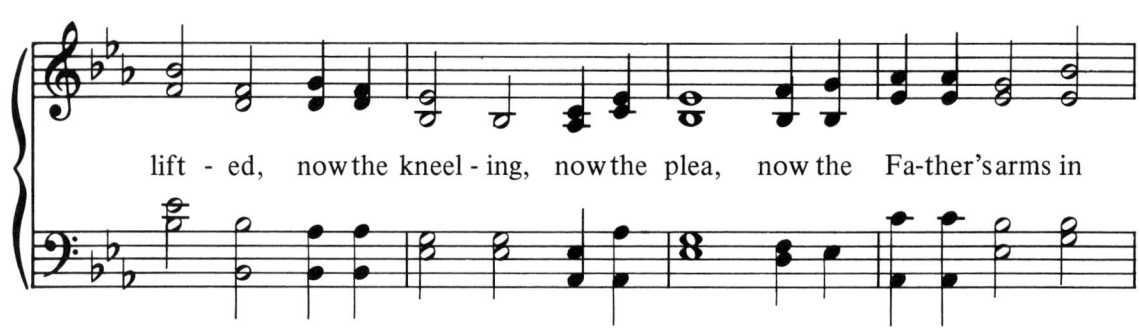

lift - ed, now the kneel - ing, now the plea, now the Fa-ther's arms in

wel - come, now the heal - ing, now the power, now the ves-sel brimmed for

rallentando

pour - ing, now the Bo - dy, now the Blood, now the joy - ful ce - le -

bra - tion, now the wed - ding, now the songs, now the heart for - giv - en

leap - ing, now the Spi - rit's vi - si - ta - tion, now the Son's e - pi - phan -

y, now the Fa - ther's bless - ing, now, __ now, __ now.

29

Start again

NEWSTART

♩ = 120

1 This man who had pa-ral-y-sis, a pris'-ner on his bed, was

feel-ing use-less,— wished that he were dead. He

had four friends who stood by him and held him in their love; at

Je-sus' feet they lowered him from a-bove. *Refrain* 'Rise *for now you're*

free;   *rise,*   *for now you're*   *free.'*

Je - sus said to   *that bound man,*   *'Start*   *a - gain with*   *me.'*

2   A man once lived among the tombs,
and Legion was his name;
he frightened folk, till one day Jesus came.
In panic Legion rushed at him
and gashed himself with stones,
but Jesus stood, and spoke in gentle tones:
    'Peace now, do not fear,' (twice)
    Jesus said to Legion then,
    'Start again from here.'

4   A fit took hold upon a boy
and hurled him to the ground;
his father cried, 'O, can no cure be found?'
The doctors tried, but all their skill
could do no good at all;
then Jesus came, and heard the father's call:
    'Let your worry cease,' (twice)
    said Jesus to that father's boy,
    'Start again in peace.'

3   'Blind man,' they said to Bartimaeus,
'stop shouting and be quiet.'
He cried still louder, 'Jesus, give me sight!'
When Jesus heard, he stopped and said,
'Who calls out for my care?'
The blind man stumbled up to Jesus there:
    'Go, and see your way,' (twice)
    Jesus said to Bartimaeus,
    'Start again today.'

5   The children of Jerusalem,
who sang your praises then,
rejoiced because you brought new life to
Today we too are glad to sing   [them.
our praises to you, Lord;
your friends, your Bible, speak to us your
    'Life is meant to be   [word:
    full and gay and free.
    I'm your Lord, and I'm your life;
    start again with me.'

Roland Giese

30

Father of night

for Bev Sutherland

NIGHTSONG

♩ = 104

1 Fa-ther of night, fa-ther of day, fa-ther who tak-eth the dark-ness a-way, fa-ther who teach-eth the birds to fly, build-er of rain-bows_ up in the sky, fa-ther of lone-li-ness and pain, fa-ther of love, and fa-ther of rain.

2 Fa - ther of day, fa - ther of night, fa - ther of black,

fa - ther of white, fa - ther who builds up the mountain so high, who

shap-eth the cloud up in the sky, fa - ther of time,

fa - ther of dreams, fa-ther who turn - eth the riv - ers and streams.

3 Fa - ther of grain, fa - ther of wheat, fa - ther of cold and __

fa - ther of heat, fa - ther of air and__ fa -ther of trees, who

dwells in our hearts and our mem - o - ries, fa -ther of min - utes,

fa - ther of days, fa - ther of whom we most sol - emn-ly praise.

✦ 31 ✦
I am the great sun

NORMANDY

♩ = 88

1 I am the great sun, but you do not see me; I am your

hus-band, but you turn a - way. I am the cap - tive, but you do not

*

vv.1.2. v.3

free me; I am the cap-tain you will not o - bey. slay.

3 I am your life, but if you will not name me, seal up your

soul with tears and nev-er blame me. wife, your child,

*Verse two, bar ten

1   I am the great sun, but you do not see me;
I am your husband, but you turn away.
I am the captive, but you do not free me;
I am the captain you will not obey.

2   I am the truth, but you will not believe me;
I am the city where you will not stay.
I am your wife, your child, but you will leave me;
I am that God to whom you will not pray.

3   I am your counsel, but you do not hear me;
I am the lover whom you will betray.
I am the victor, but you do not cheer me;
I am the holy dove whom you will slay.
I am your life, but if you will not name me,
seal up your soul with tears, and never blame me.

Charles Causley

◈ 32 ◈
Pentecost

for Sue Langley

DOVE DANCE

1 So free, so bright, so beau-ti-ful and fair, the

Ho — ly Dove de -scends the earth- ly air: in start - ling

joy -ance come from its im - mor-tal home, it bears the

glo — ry that we all __ may share. __

Verse four, bars ten to thirteen

al - ways there de - scend - ing, al - ways there a - scend - ing, it

2 Through ancient space and newest time,
   it brings transcendent reason to a world of
   it shows each mind and heart   [things:
   how to assume its part
   in dances born of God's imaginings.

3 On wings of subtlest flame, the Holy Dove
   flies through the human world and offers
   it teaches heart and mind   [love:
   how to transcend their kind
   and praise the God who lets all being move.

4 So free, so bright, so beautiful and fair,
   the Holy Dove flies through the mortal air:
   always there descending,
   always there ascending,
   it brings the glory that we all may share.

                                    John Bennett

❖ 33 ❖
Jesus thy boundless love

MARCUS ♩ = 120

1 Je - sus, thy bound-less love to me   O   knit my thank-ful
no thought can reach, no tongue de-clare;

heart to thee,   and   reign with - out   a   ri - val there: thine

whol - ly, thine a - lone I   am; be   thou a - lone my   con-stant flame.

1   Jesus, thy boundless love to me
    no thought can reach, no tongue declare;
    O knit my thankful heart to thee,
    and reign without a rival there:
    thine wholly, thine alone I am;
    be thou alone my constant flame.

2   From all eternity, with love
    unchangeable thou hast me viewed;
    ere knew this beating heart to move,
    thy tender mercies me pursued:
    ever with me thy love abide,
    and close me in on every side.

3   O grant that nothing in my soul
    may dwell, but thy pure love alone;
    O may thy love possess me whole,
    my joy, my treasure, and my crown:
    strange fires far from my heart remove;
    my every act, word, thought, be love.

4   Still let thy love point out my way;
    how wondrous things thy love has wrought!
    Still lead me, lest I go astray;
    direct my word, inspire my thought;
    and if I fall, soon may I hear
    thy voice, and know that love is near.

5   In suffering be thy love my peace,
    in weakness my almighty power;
    and when the storm of life shall cease,
    Jesus, in that important hour,
    in death as life be thou my guide,
    and save me, who for me has died.

Paul Gerhadt, trans. John Wesley

83

◇ 34 ◇
Eternal Spirit of the living Christ

for Andrew Doubleday

ARGYLE STREET

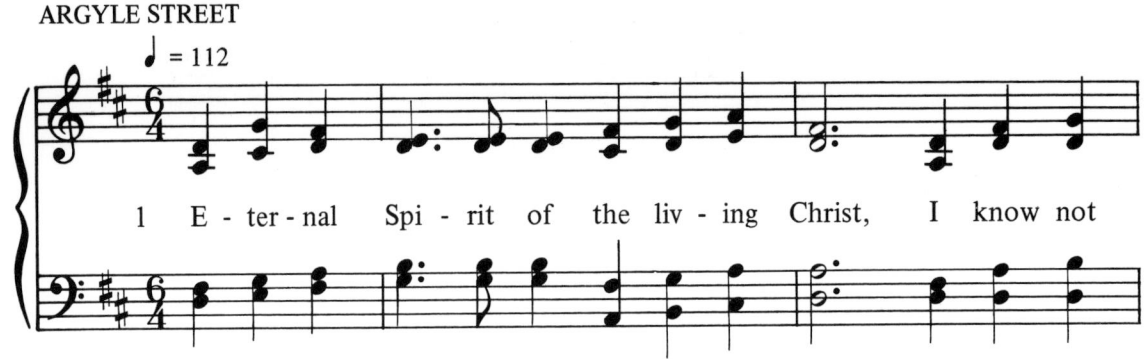

1 E - ter - nal Spi - rit of the liv - ing Christ, I know not

how to ask, or what to say; I on - ly know my need, as deep as

life, and on - ly you can teach me how to pray.

1   Eternal Spirit of the living Christ,
    I know not how to ask, or what to say;
    I only know my need, as deep as life,
    and only you can teach me how to pray.

2   Come, pray in me the prayer I need this day;
    help me to see your purpose and your will —
    where I have failed, what I have done amiss;
    held in forgiving love, let me be still.

3   Come with the vision and the strength I need
    to serve my God, and all humanity;
    fulfillment of my life in love outpoured —
    my life in you, O Christ, your love in me.

Frank von Christenson

◈ **35** ◈
Prayer of protection

SOMERSET

♩ = 120

1 First come Lord God, and then come Ho - ly

Ghost, and then come sweet Je - su, and

then come sweet Je - su, who died, and

1 First come Lord God,
   and then come Holy Ghost,
   and then come sweet Jesu,
   and then come sweet Jesu,
   who died, and rose,
   and loves us all the most.

2 Bless us Lord God,
   and blessed Trinity,
   and bless us sweet Jesu,
   and bless us sweet Jesu,
   who guards us all,
   wherever we may be.

3 Glory to God,
   and praise the Trinity,
   and praise little Jesu,
   who slept in a manger,
   who died, and rose,
   through love for you and me.

Somerset carol

◈ 36 ◈
Young beam of heaven

SHINING

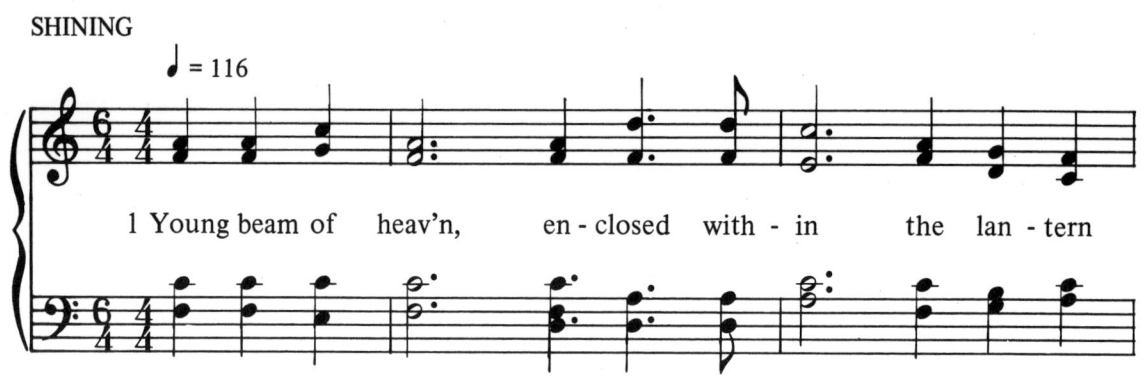

1 Young beam of heav'n, en - closed with - in the lan - tern

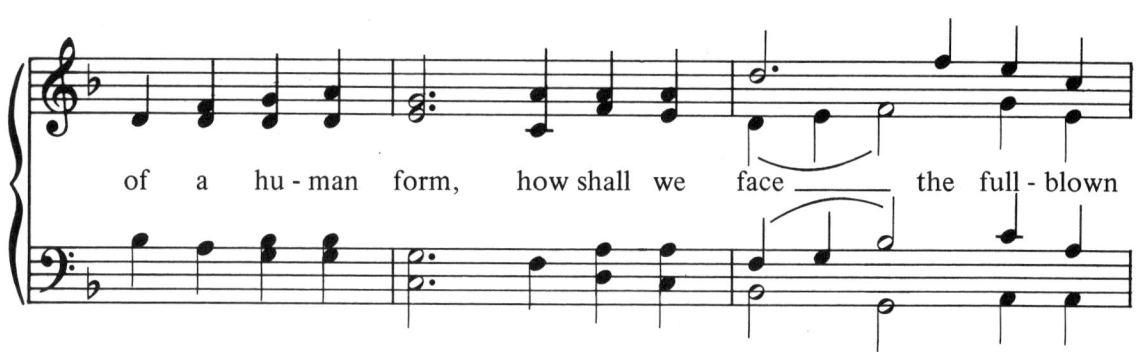

of a hu - man form, how shall we face ____ the full - blown

light, ____ who find the bud too sharp ____ for sight?

1   Young beam of heaven, enclosed within
      the lantern of a human form,
      how shall we face the full-blown light,
      who find the bud too sharp for sight?

2   All brilliance known to human eyes —
    white light of winter-burning skies,
    gold light that gives the green its glow
    and makes a rose of sullen snow —

3   All these, the blessed lights of earth,
    are little candles to his birth:
    too bright to bear, but that he could
    find means to make our weakness good.

4   Our darkness gives his light its place,
    our darkness gives a Prince his peace:
    he puts his life within our hands,
    and in that cradle sleeps, and shines.

Anne Ridler

37
Unto us a Son is given

MEYNELL

1 Giv - en, not lent, and not with - drawn once sent, this

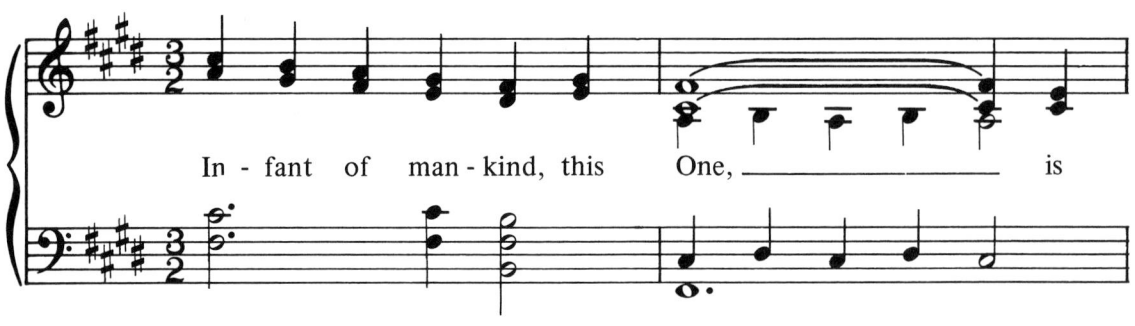

In - fant of man - kind, this One, _____ is

still the lit - tle wel - come Son. _____

1   Given, not lent,
    and not withdrawn — once sent,
    this Infant of mankind, this One,
    is still the little welcome Son.

2   New every year,
    new born and newly dear,
    he comes with tidings and a song,
    the ages long, the ages long.

3   Ev'n as the cold
    keen winter grows not old,
    as childhood is so fresh, foreseen,
    and spring in the familiar green.

4   Sudden as sweet
    come the expected feet.
    All joy is young, and new all art,
    and he, too, whom we have by heart.

Alice Meynell

◇ 38 ◇
A stable lamp is lighted

for Evan Lewis

SPRINGHILL

1 A sta - ble lamp_ is light - ed whose glow shall wake_ the

sky,____ the stars shall bend their voi - ces, and ev - ery stone shall

cry:____ and ev - ery stone shall cry,____ and straw like gold shall

shine;____ a barn shall har-bour heav - en, a stall_become a shrine.__

1 A stable lamp is lighted whose glow shall wake the sky,
the stars shall bend their voices, and every stone shall cry:
and every stone shall cry, and straw like gold shall shine;
a barn shall harbour heaven, a stall become a shrine.

2 This child through David's city shall ride in triumph by;
the palm shall strew its branches, and every stone shall cry:
and every stone shall cry, though heavy, dull, and dumb,
and lie within the roadway to pave his kingdom come.

3 Yet he shall be forsaken and yielded up to die;
the sky shall groan and darken, and every stone shall cry:
and every stone shall cry for stony hearts of men;
God's blood upon the spearhead, God's love refused again.

4 But now, as at the ending, the low is lifted high;
the stars shall bend their voices, and every stone shall cry:
and every stone shall cry in praises of the child
by whose descent among us the worlds are reconciled.

Richard Wilbur

Three masts has the thrusting ship

for Tim and Alan

THREE MASTS

1 Three masts has the thrust-ing ship; three masts will she wear, when she, like Christ our Sav - iour, walks on the wat - 'ry stair.

The rhythm of this hymn is irregular. Verses 2 to 5 are to be sung as follows:

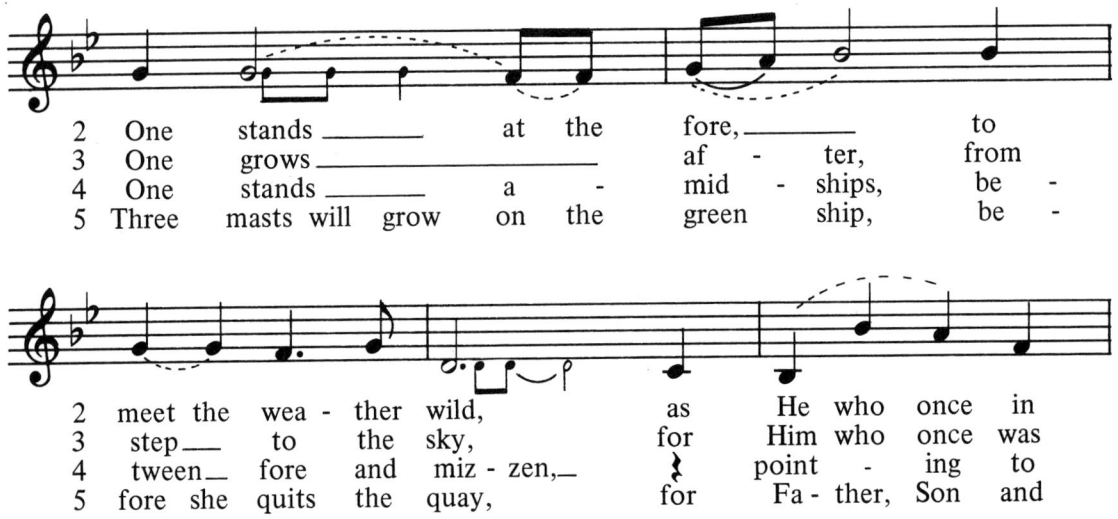

2	One	stands		at	the	fore,		to		
3	One	grows			af -	ter,		from		
4	One	stands		a -	mid -	ships,		be -		
5	Three	masts will	grow	on	the	green	ship,	be -		

2	meet the	wea -	ther	wild,	as	He who	once	in	
3	step	to	the	sky,	for	Him who	once	was	
4	tween	fore	and	miz - zen,	for	point -	ing	to	
5	fore she	quits	the	quay,	for	Fa - ther,	Son	and	

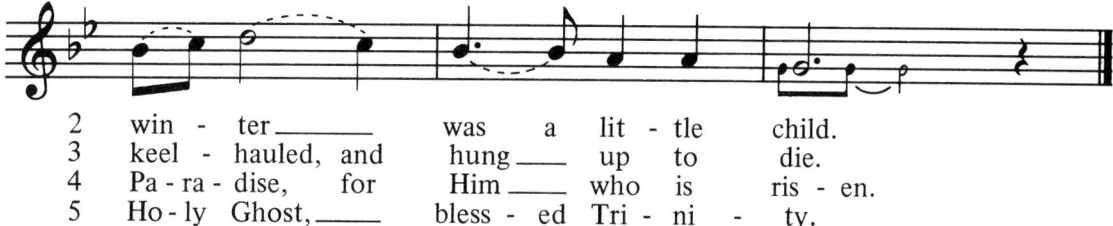

2	win - ter ____	was	a	lit - tle	child.
3	keel - hauled, and	hung ____	up	to	die.
4	Pa - ra - dise,	for	Him ____	who	is	ris - en.
5	Ho - ly Ghost, ____	bless - ed	Tri - ni	-	ty.

1 Three masts has the thrusting ship;
three masts will she wear,
when she, like Christ our Saviour,
walks on the watery stair.

2 One stands at the fore,
to meet the weather wild,
as He who once in winter
was a little child.

3 One grows after,
from step to the sky,
for Him who once was keel-hauled,
and hung up to die.

4 One stands amidships,
between fore and mizzen,
pointing to Paradise,
for Him who is risen.

5 Three masts will grow on the green ship,
before she quits the quay,
for Father, Son and Holy Ghost,
blessed Trinity.

Charles Causley

Note. Step: mast support; keel-hauled: savagely punished; mizzen: rear sail.

◈ **40** ◈
A New Zealand carol

1 Ca - rol our Christ - mas, an up - side down Christ - mas;

snow is not fall - ing and trees are not bare.

Ca - rol the sum - mer, and wel - come the Christ Child,

warm in our sun - shine and sweet - ness of air.

1 Carol our Christmas, an upside down Christmas;
   snow is not falling, and trees are not bare.
   Carol the summer, and welcome the Christ Child,
   warm in our sunshine and sweetness of air.

2 Sing of the gold and the green and the sparkle,
   water and river and lure of the beach.
   Sing in the happiness of open spaces,
   sing a nativity summer can reach!

3 Shepherds and musterers move over hillsides,
   finding, not angels, but sheep to be shorn;
   wise ones make journeys, whatever the season,
   searching for signs of the truth to be born.

4 Right side up Christmas belongs to the universe,
   made in the moment a woman gives birth;
   hope is the Jesus gift, love is the offering,
   everywhere, anywhere, here on the earth.

Shirley Murray

❖ 41 ❖
Carol for a New Zealand child

for Theo Gibson

THEO

1 Christ - mas in the pic - ture book, all gold and white with
2 car - ol ba - by Je - sus on a nor' west

1 snow; win - ter in the des - ert, where the three Kings
2 day; a sum - mer wind is blow - ing a - cross the beach and

1 go. Ice on the cam - el rein, rime on the
2 bay. Sea - gulls are wheel - ing where the child - ren run to

1 crown;   snow   a - round the   sta - ble doors,
2 swim;   laugh - ter in   the   break   -   ers,

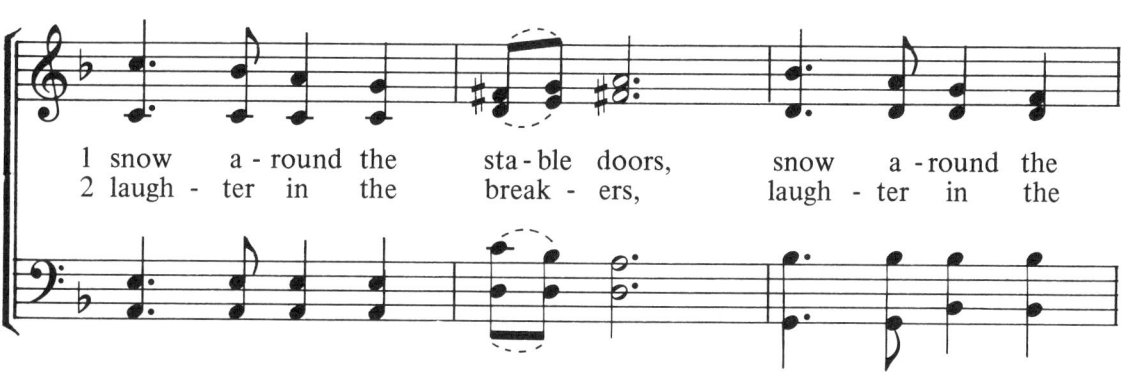

1 snow   a - round the   sta - ble doors,   snow   a - round the
2 laugh - ter in   the   break   -   ers,   laugh - ter in   the

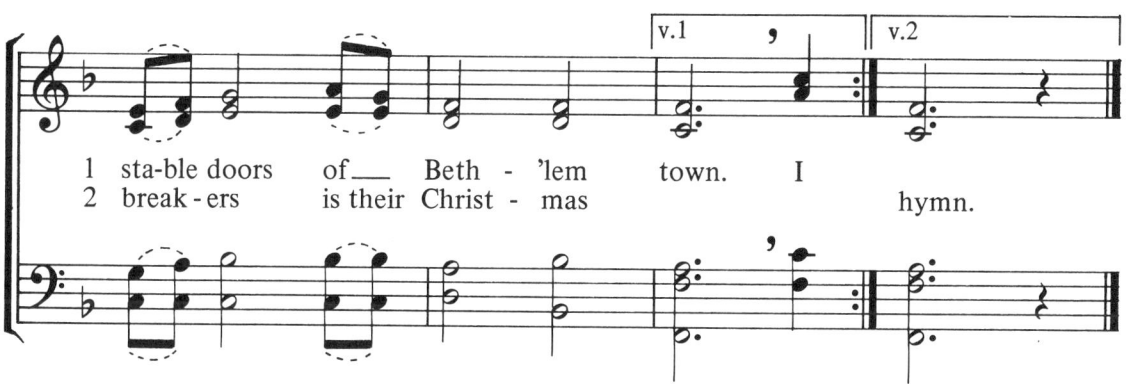

1 sta-ble doors   of __ Beth - 'lem   town.   I
2 break - ers   is their Christ - mas   hymn.

◈ 42 ◈
Children's Christmas hymn

1   And did you see him, little star,
    long, long ago?
    And was it you, I wonder, shone
    on manger low?
    And did you see the shepherd men,
    when angels sang?
    'Peace on the earth, good-will to all,'
    the message rang.

2   And did you guide the three wise kings
    with shining light?
    And bring them to the holy Child
    on that great night?
    And will you still shine down on earth,
    though from afar,
    and lead us back to Bethlehem,
    O little star?

Helen D. Clyde

43

The first night

BLESSING

Quickly and lightly ♩. = 112

1 In the deep De - cem - ber night, when each sand - alled wind was
to the listen-ing ear of earth spoke the bell - bird from the

still,_____
hill._____

2 'O my bub - bling peal of bells,

O my lit - tle mel - o - dy, let me chime your

com - ing in, let me bless__ you from__ a tree.'

1   In the deep December night,
       when each sandalled wind was still,
       to the listening ear of earth
       spoke the bellbird from the hill.

2 'O my bubbling peal of bells,
   O my little melody,
   let me chime your coming in,
   let me bless you from a tree.'

3 Said the hihi, glowing gold:
   'With my stitch that comes and goes,
   O my naked little Christ,
   let me stitch your bits of clothes!'

4 Said the bittern, booming deep:
   'Little soldier, in that night
   when the spears shall crowd you thick,
   let me drum your foes to flight.'

5 And the tern, with sailor wing:
   'Little salt, who'll choose to be
   friend of all poor fishermen,
   take a blessing from the sea.'

6 Sang the tui – God, how clear! –
   'Little love, oh, come away!
   Come into the bush tonight;
   we will love you more than they.'

7 So into the quiet dripped
   the great tender, fluting words,
   and a cross of stars burned blue
   at the blessing of the birds.

Note Hihi: stitchbird.

Eileen Duggan

44
Carol

GERALDINE *for Dorothy Pearce*

1 Come to this Christ - mas sing - ing! Come to this
birth - day, bring - ing gifts from our coun - try's
trea - sures, beau - ty of shell __ and stone.
Wis - dom the old __ have taught us, laugh - ter the

104

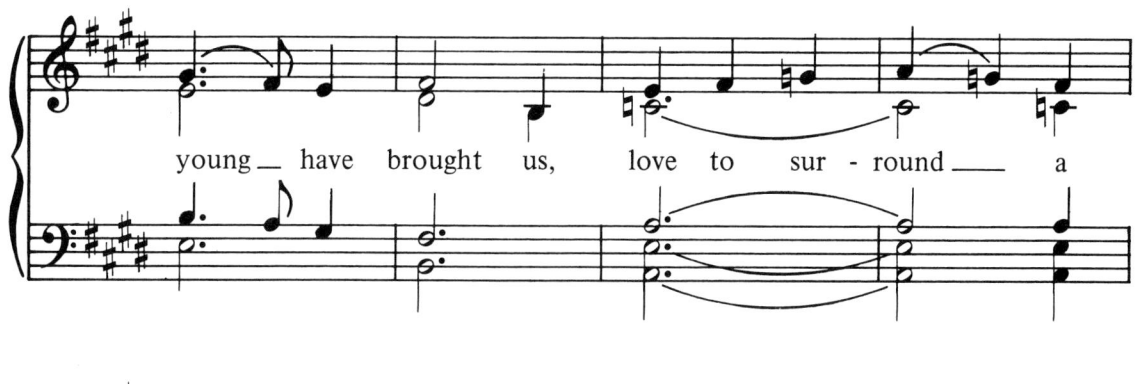

young — have brought us, love to sur - round — a

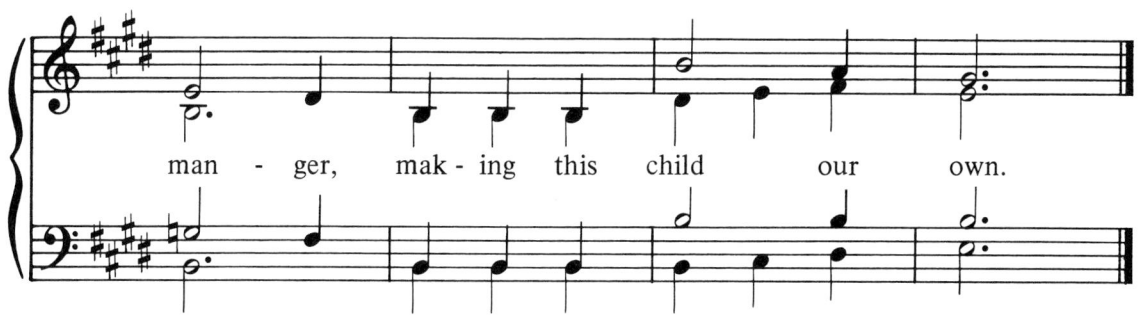

man - ger, mak - ing this child our own.

1 Come to this Christmas singing!
   come to this birthday, bringing
   gifts from our country's treasures,
   beauty of shell and stone.
        Wisdom the old have taught us,
        laughter the young have brought us,
        love to surround a manger,
        making this Child our own.

2 Wealth of our land and water,
   riches of race and culture —
   these be our gold and incense,
   offered for Christmas Day.
        Where we make peace, declare it,
        where we have much, to share it;
        aroha warm our hearts, and
        aroha be our way.

3 Here where the sheep are grazing,
   where summer sun is blazing,
   harvests for others ripen —
   food for the world can grow.
        Christ of a cold December,
        quicken us to remember
        poverty in a stable,
        need, like the sting of snow.

Note Aroha: love.

Shirley Murray

45

I read your signature

HERIOT ROW

♩ = 108

I read your sig-na-ture in the rose, and in the rock and the

fab-ling sea, and fol-low through ev-'ry when and where the

lines of your face and the print of your hand. Yet write for me sharp-er on

eye and ear your form and name, my liv-ing bread,

that I may nev-er go hun-gry more, but ev-en in the farth-est

gal-ler-ies of air wake and sleep_____ as though in your hand.

I read your signature in the rose,
and in the rock and the fabling sea,
and follow through every when and where
the lines of your face and the print of your hand.
Yet write for me sharper on eye and ear
your form and name, my living bread,
that I may never go hungry more,
but even in the farthest galleries of air
wake and sleep as though in your hand.

Charles Brasch

SONGS FOR YOUNG PEOPLE

✧ 46 ✧
A song of Abraham

PROMISED LAND

American folk melody

1 The Lord said to A-bra-ham, 'leave your own na-tive land, leave all your kins-folk, too. _____ Go forth to a coun-try far a-way; I will bless, I will hon-our you.'

2   'No need to be frightened; why, look up into the sky,
number the stars, if you can,
and so many shall your children be,
sons and daughters of Abraham.'

3   Then Abram, with no delay, set out upon his way,
travelling the desert sand.
With Sarah his wife, and his nephew Lot,
he is bound for a promised land.

4   But one hot and thirsty day three travellers came his way;
'under the shade of this tree,'
Abram said, 'take your rest, and be my guest,
share my food and my drink with me.'

5   The Lord, through those angel-men, spoke to his servant then:
'Sarah will bear you a son!'
How those parents were glad with their tiny lad;
called him Isaac, the Laughing One.

6   But God tested Abraham, asked him to slay his lamb;
sadly he stooped to obey.
'You are tested and tried; put your knife aside,
for such faith you are blest this day.'

7   O make us like Abram, Lord, swift to obey your word,
faithful to follow your plan;
and like him we will go to the place you show,
we will march out like Abraham.

◇ **47** ◇
A song of David

PONT D'AVIGNON
French folk melody (adapted)

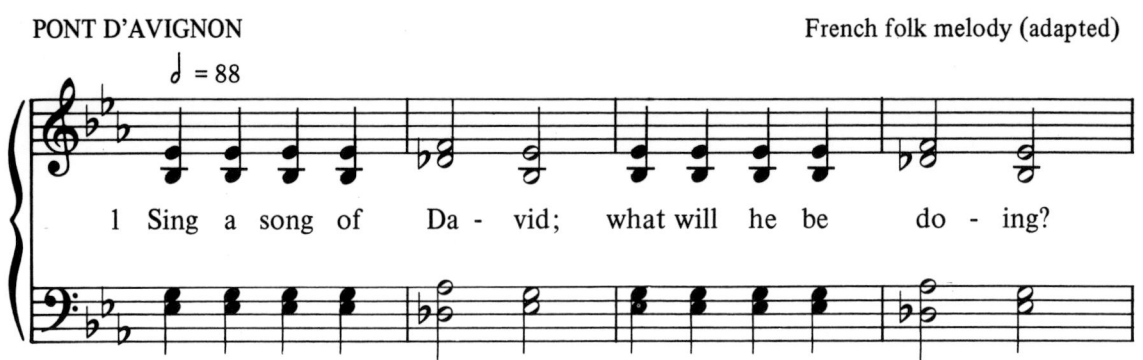

1 Sing a song of Da - vid; what will he be do - ing?

He'll take care not one bear drags a lamb off to its lair.

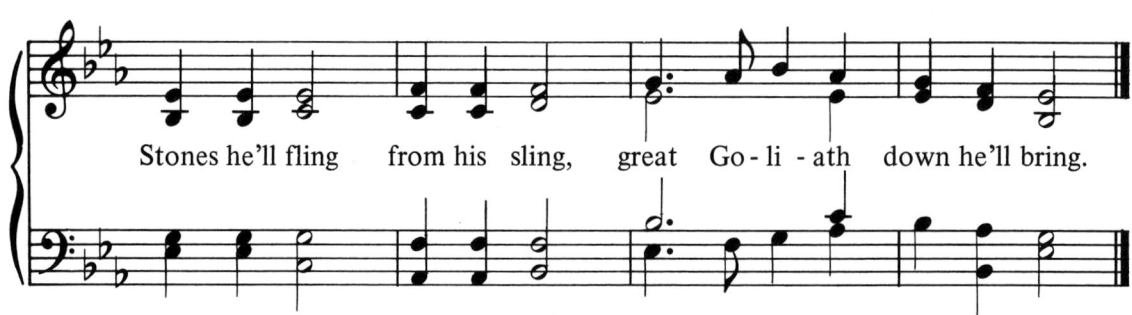

Stones he'll fling from his sling, great Go - li - ath down he'll bring.

1 Sing a song of David;
  what will he be doing?
  He'll take care not one bear
  drags a lamb off to its lair.
  Stones he'll fling from his sling,
  great Goliath down he'll bring.

2 Just a boy, young David;
  what will he be doing?
  All life through he'll be true,
  Jonathan, his friend, to you.
  Run away; night and day
  Saul will seek his life to slay.

3 Sing the praise of David,
  champion of Israel.
  Just you see; he will be
  crowned the king, His Majesty.
  He will fight in God's might
  for his people and the right.

4 Sing the praise of David,
  mighty King of Judah.
  Take he will Zion's hill,
  raise a city famous still.
  Rule begun, Jesse's son
  making all the nation one.

5 Sing the grief of David;
  good and bad in David.
  Here comes strife to his life
  when he steals Uriah's wife.
  Time runs by; he will cry
  'Absalom!' His son must die.

6 Sing the songs of David,
  shepherd king of Israel.
  Psalms he raised all his days,
  serving God, the God we praise.
  Trumpets ring, harp and string,
  David's life for God we sing.

◇ 48 ◇
The four evangelists

GOSPEL WRITERS

1 Mat-thew, Mark and Luke and John took a pen and_ wrote it down,

all the sto-ries they had heard, ev-ery deed and_ ev-ery word.

See how a moth-er mild wel-comes Christ, her_ lit-tle child;

see, with the ris-ing sun, on the beach the_ Ris-en One.

Refrain

Mat-thew, Mark and Luke and John, send-ing news of_ Je-sus on.

1 Matthew, Mark and Luke and John
took a pen and wrote it down,
all the stories they had heard,
every deed and every word.
See how a mother mild
welcomes Christ, her little child;
see, with the rising sun,
on the beach the Risen One.
    Matthew, Mark and Luke and John,
    sending news of Jesus on.

2 God is with us, Matthew said,
there he lies on a manger bed;
Christ the King, of David's line,
with us to the end of time;
doing his Father's will,
God's great purpose to fulfill;
calling to righteousness,
taking bread and wine to bless.

3 Peter told young Mark, his friend,
how he loved them to the end,
how he made the cripple strong,
how he broke the power of wrong.
Blind folk he made to see,
Son of Man, in majesty;
dying, he set us free,
Christ the Lord, eternally.

4 Doctor Luke set down with care
Jesus' life of praise and prayer;
told the world that he had come
loving, serving everyone;
calmed down a raging sea,
called Zacchaeus from his tree,
shared Martha's busy home,
praised the faith of the man of Rome.

5 John, at last, took eagle flight,
saw the Christ with eagle sight;
saw the glory of the Lord,
knew him for God's mighty Word.
Jesus, the living vine,
light that will for ever shine,
grace, truth in God's dear son,
he who seeks to make us one.
    Matthew, Mark and Luke and John,
    we will send your glad news on.

◈ 49 ◈
Seek and you shall find

SEEKING

1 When the for - ty days were ov - er, Cap - tain

No - ah looked a - bout. All a - round him lay the

wa - ters, so he sent a ra - ven out. When the

ra - ven brought no mes - sage, No - ah took a dove in hand, and that

snow-white dove kept search - ing till it found dry land.

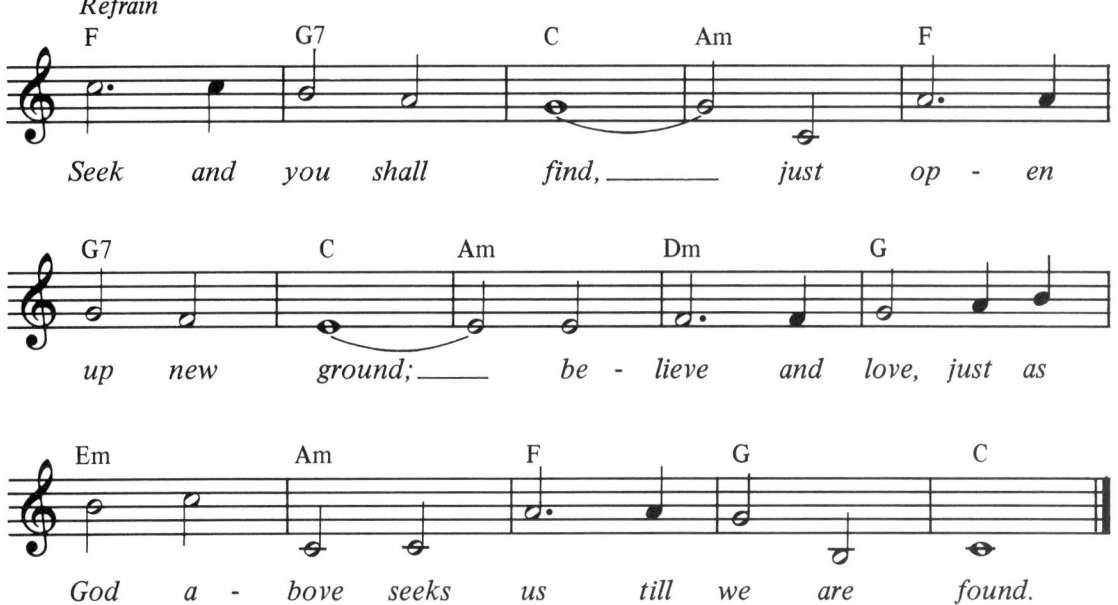

Refrain

Seek and you shall find, _____ just op - en
up new ground; _____ be - lieve and love, just as
God a - bove seeks us till we are found.

1 When the forty days were over Captain Noah looked about.
   All around him lay the waters, so he sent a raven out.
   When the raven brought no message, Noah took a dove in hand,
   and that snow-white dove kept searching till it found dry land.
       Seek and you shall find,
       just open up new ground;
       believe and love, just as God above
       seeks us till we are found.

2 Can you see that rich young fellow walking sadly on his way:
   he was looking for a new life, till he found he had to pay.
   'I have kept the ten commandments, I have followed every law.'
   Jesus looked at him and loved him: 'There is one thing more.'

3 Once a girl who owned ten sovereigns lost one somewhere in her room,
   so she lit up all the candles, set to sweeping with a broom;
   looked in each and every corner, till she found it hiding there,
   then she called in all the friends she knew, her joy to share.

4 Very early in the morning they went sadly to the tomb
   where Christ Jesus had been buried, and they found an empty room.
   'You must look among the living, for you will not find him here;
   Christ is risen and among you; he is everywhere.'

◈ **50** ◈

Sing, sing, and what shall we sing?

RIGHTEOUS MAN

English folk song

1 Sing, sing, and what shall we sing? Sing all o - ver one, and

Refrain

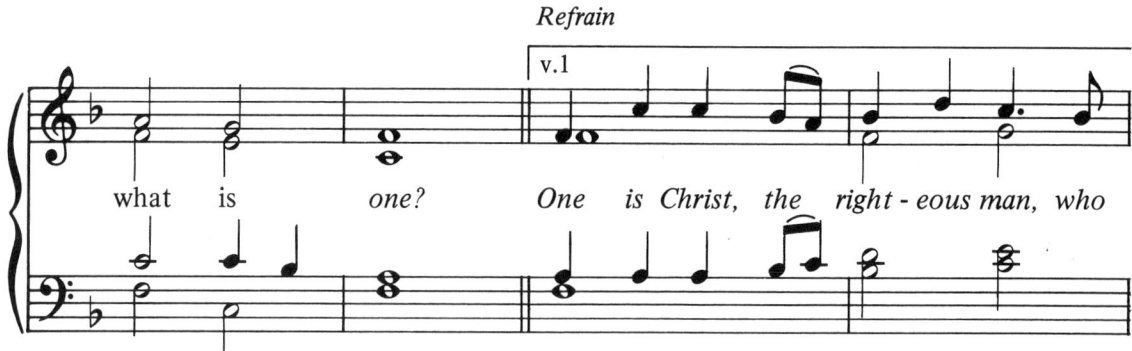

what is one? One is Christ, the right - eous man, who

saved our souls to rest, a - men. . Two is the fish - er crew,

* This bar is repeated as often as required to include all the numbers as they are added,
one at a time, in the course of the song.

One is Christ the right-eous man who saved our souls to rest, a-men.

Sing, sing, and what shall we sing?
Sing all over *one,* and what is *one?*
One is Christ, the righteous man,
who saved our souls to rest, amen.

Two is the fisher crew.

Three is the Trinity.

Four is the open door.

Five is the man alive.

Six is the crucifix.

Seven is the love of heaven.

Eight is the crooked straight.

Nine is the bread and wine.

Ten, he will come again.

◇ **51** ◇

The helper

THE BALLAD OF HENRY MARTIN

Ho - ly Spi - rit, Help - er, come to us now. _____ now.

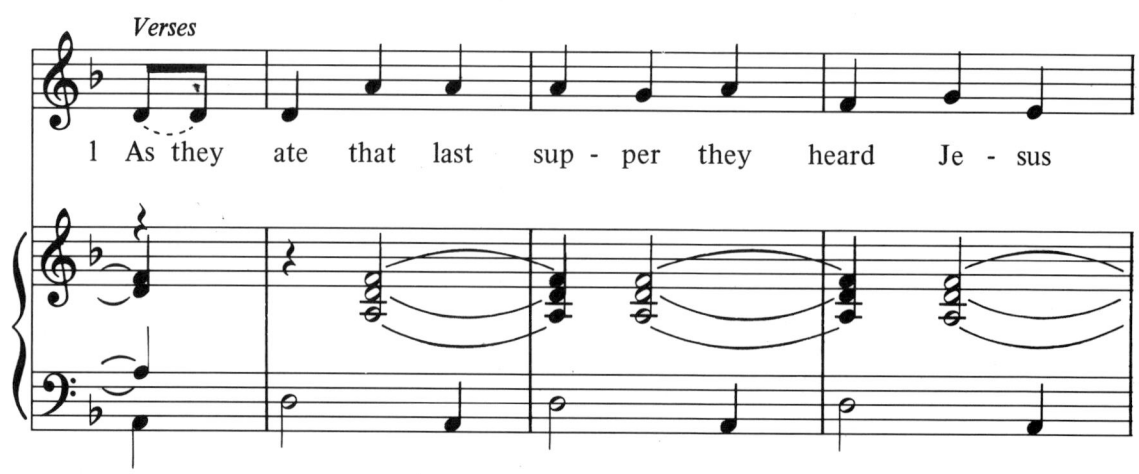

1 As they ate that last sup - per they heard Je - sus

say, 'It is bet-ter for you that I go.'_____ 'No,'

said his dis - ci - ples, 'that can-not be true,___ that can-not be

D.C. al Fine

true.' 'But a Help - er,' said Je - sus, 'I'm send - ing to you.'

Verses continued overleaf

Holy Spirit, Helper, come to us now.

1 As they ate that last supper they heard Jesus say,
   'It is better for you that I go.'
   'No,' said his disciples, 'that cannot be true,
      that cannot be true.'
   'But a Helper,' said Jesus, 'I'm sending to you.'

2 Wherever they are, Jesus' friends understand
   that the Helper he promised is near.
   The Spirit is with us; unseen and unheard,
      unseen and unheard,
   he helps us to know and obey Jesus' word.

3 Disciples of Jesus, we meet here today;
   we will learn how to follow our Lord.
   The Spirit will help us, as Jesus has said,
      as Jesus has said;
   a fire in our hearts, and a light where we tread.

Roland Giese

◇ 52 ◇

Psalm 151

TOOTING

To be played and sung briskly ♩ = 92

1 With a hoot and a toot on a pipe — or a flute we will

praise, we will wor - ship God; — with a hum or a thrum, with a

Refrain

roll — on a drum, we will make him a joy - ful noise. *Bow a*

cel - lo that is mel - low, sound a trum - pet call, *blow a*

horn and a deep_ bas - soon; ev-ery in-stru-ment is play -ing, with our

firmly

voi- ces we are say - ing we re - joice, we are glad in God.

Optional alternative verse 2 opening.

A little slower

2 With a flat or a sharp, with a chord_ on a harp, we will

in time again

praise, we will wor - ship God;_____

Sound effects should be added wherever possible.

124

1 With a hoot and a toot
on a pipe or a flute
we will praise, we will worship God;
with a hum or a thrum,
with a roll on a drum,
we will make him a joyful noise.
Bow a cello that is mellow
sound a trumpet call,
blow a horn and a deep bassoon;
every instrument is playing,
with our voices we are saying
we rejoice, we are glad in God.

2 With a flat or a sharp,
with a chord on a harp,
we will praise, we will worship God;
with a ping on a string,
with a choir that can sing,
we will make him a joyful noise.

3 With the clap of a hand,
or the sound of a band,
we will praise, we will worship God;
with a paper and comb,
on an old trombone,
we will make him a joyful noise.

4 With a peal on a bell,
with a cheer or a yell,
we will praise, we will worship God;
with a bong on a gong,
through the words of this song,
we will make him a joyful noise.

53

Father forgive

ROLAND

This song may be sung as a unison melody, or as a simple two-part canon (as set out here).

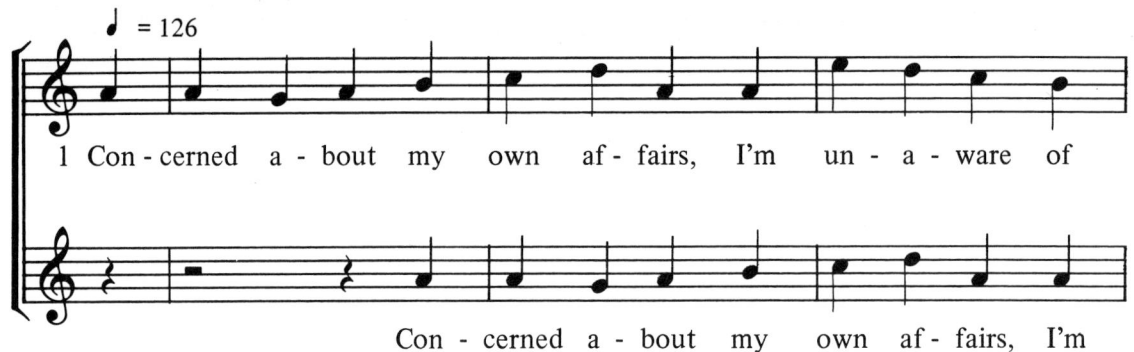

1 Con - cerned a - bout my own af - fairs, I'm un - a - ware of

Con - cerned a - bout my own af - fairs, I'm

oth - ers' cares. I give my word, 'Yes, count me in,' but

un - a - ware of oth - ers' cares. I give my word, 'Yes

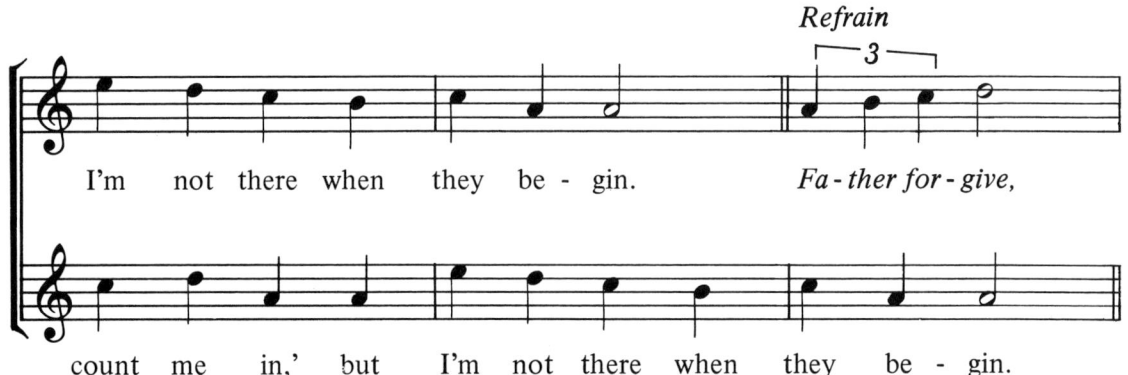

I'm not there when they be - gin. *Fa - ther for - give,*

count me in,' but I'm not there when they be - gin.

help me to live   as a true friend would. _____

Fa - ther for-give,   help me to live   as a true friend would.

1   Concerned about my own affairs,
    I'm unaware of others' cares.
    I give my word, 'Yes, count me in,'
    but I'm not there when they begin.
        Father forgive,
        help me to live
        as a true friend would.

2   A friend suggests a plan for fun;
    unwilling, I've a better one.
    But Jesus said, 'The way friends take
    is giving self for others' sake.'

                                    Roland Giese

54

How much am I worth?

LANGLEY

♩ = 168

1 How much am I worth? What val - ue's in me? Do I

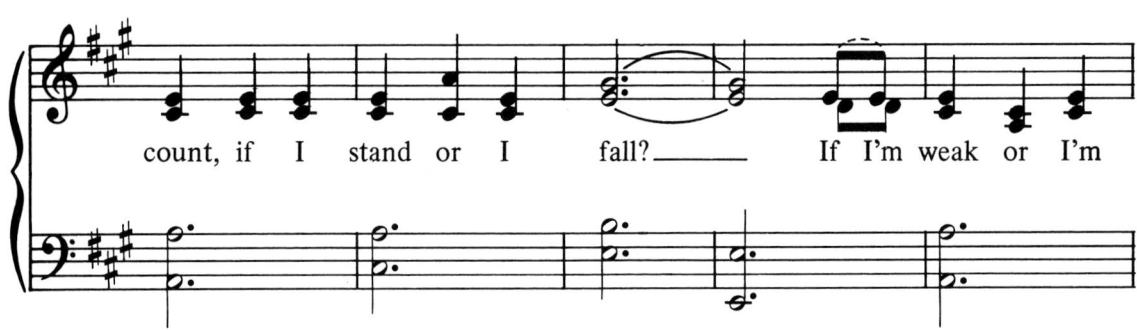

count, if I stand or I fall?_____ If I'm weak or I'm

strong, if I win or I lose, am I some - one, or

no one at all?_____ *I am worth ev-ery-thing,*
You are worth ev-ery-thing,

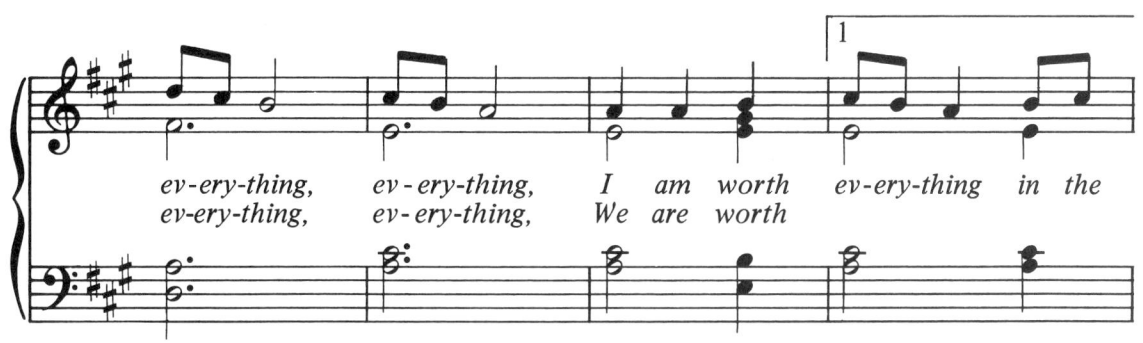

ev-ery-thing,   ev-ery-thing,   I   am   worth   ev-ery-thing   in   the
ev-ery-thing,   ev-ery-thing,   We   are   worth

eyes   of   God;

ev-ery-thing in the eyes   of   God.

Verses continued overleaf

1 How much am I worth? What value's in me?
   Do I count, if I stand or I fall?
   If I'm weak or I'm strong, if I win or I lose,
   am I someone, or no one at all?
       I am worth everything, everything, everything,
       I am worth everything in the eyes of God;
       you are worth everything, everything, everything,
       we are worth everything in the eyes of God.

2 I am that bird that dropped to the ground,
   the tiniest bird of them all,
   and nobody knew, and nobody cared,
   but our Father, who cares for us all.
       We are worth everything, everything, everything,
       we are worth everything in the eyes of God;
       you are worth everything, everything, everything,
       we are worth everything in the eyes of God.

3 I am that stone that fell from a ring,
   that was precious beyond all compare;
   and they hunted the house, till they cried out with joy
   when they saw it, still gleaming, down there.

4 I am that child who felt lost and afraid,
   when she saw just how far she had roamed;
   but they scoured the hills till they found her again,
   and, rejoicing, they brought her safe home.

5 How much am I worth? Do I matter at all?
   When I'm thinking it through may I see
   that I'm worth all the love of the Son of God,
   who laid down his life just for me.

55

Caring

1 'Click, click,' how the need - les fly to

knit up a jer - sey that's as warm as pie;

so God clothes us in flesh and skin,

sews on the but-tons and says 'be - gin!'

1   'Click, click,' how the needles fly
to knit up a jersey that's as warm as pie;
so God clothes us in flesh and skin,
sews on the buttons, and says 'begin!'

2   'Hush, hush,' see that little child
asleep in the arms of his mother mild;
so God shelters his family,
cares for his children, for you and me.

3   'Chick, chick,' calls the mother hen,
calls to her chickens running round the pen;
so God gathers his family,
knows my name, and calls to me.

4   'Thump, thump,' mother works the dough,
puts in the yeast to make it grow;
so God fashions his Kingdom bread,
working till all the world shall be fed.

◈ 56 ◈

I've never seen an elephant

ALL CREATURES

1 I've nev-er seen an e-le-phant, and an e-le-phant's nev-er seen me. I can't swing like a mon-key can from the branch of a trop-i-cal tree. I don't roar like a li-on does, but a li-on can't read my books;

I'm not as huge as a hip-po is, but a hip-po has-n't my

Refrain

looks. *Thank you God, thank you God, for it's*

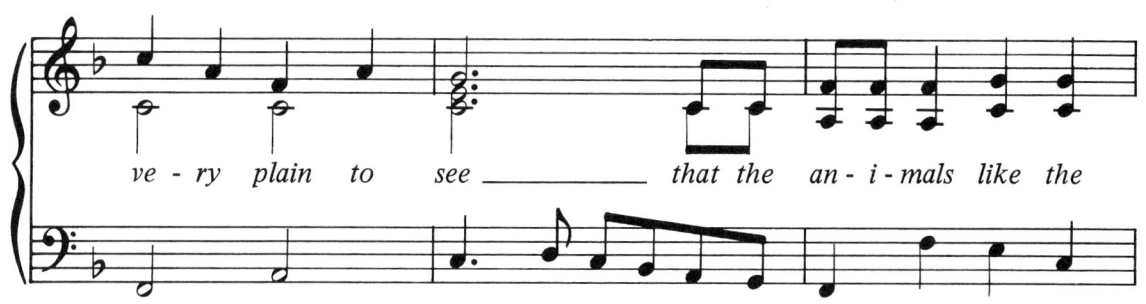

ve - ry plain to see _____ that the an - i - mals like the

way they are, and I'm glad that I like me.

1 I've never seen an elephant,
  and an elephant's never seen me.
  I can't swing like a monkey can
  from the branch of a tropical tree.
  I don't roar like a lion does,
  but a lion can't read my books;
  I'm not as huge as a hippo is,
  but a hippo hasn't my looks.
   Thank you God, thank you God,
   for it's very plain to see
   that the animals like the way they are,
   and I'm glad that I like me.

2 I've never met an octopus,
  and no octopus ever met me.
  I can't dive like a dolphin does
  through the waves of an indigo sea.
  I can't flop like a flounder can,
  or sing like a whale in the blue;
  I can't leap like a flying fish,
  but that fish can't think like I do.
   Thank you God, thank you God,
   for it's very plain to see
   that the fish all like the way they are,
   and I'm glad that I like me.

3 I've never heard a mocking-bird,
  and a mocking-bird's never heard me.
  I can't climb like a skylark climbs,
  or nest on the top of a tree.
  I don't hold what a peli-can,
  but a pelican cannot cry;
  I can dream of an aeroplane
  even though I cannot fly.
   Thank you God, thank you God,
   for it's very plain to see
   that the birds all like the way they are,
   and I'm glad that I like me.

◈ 57 ◈

Put me down for a victory crown

a hymn for the fiftieth anniversary of the Girls' Brigade in New Zealand

for Margaret Connor

TORCHLIGHT

Put me down for a vic-to-ry crown,_ here I
let me run till my jour-ney is done,_ with your

stand at the start of the race;_
wind and your sun on my face._

Make me come a-

live, _____ help me, Lord, to_ strive with

all of my might to fol - low_ you.

Put me down for a victory crown,
here I stand at the start of the race;
let me run till my journey is done,
with your wind and your sun on my face.
Make me come alive,
help me Lord, to strive
with all of my might to follow you.

1 We can be strong in the triumph song
 of the ones who have gone before,
 serving and loving God,
 seeking the risen Lord,
 finding the life evermore.

2 We will be true, in an age that is new,
 to the badge of the Cross and Flame;
 learning the truth of God,
 training to serve the world,
 bearing the sign of his name.

Acknowledgements

The Publisher's acknowledge with grateful thanks the following for permission to use copyright material:

Allen & Unwin for Eileen May Duggan 'The first night', from *New Zealand Poems,* George Allen & Unwin, London, 1940

Associated Book Publishers (U.K.) Ltd for Isaiah Sully 'Prayer of protection', from *The Chime Child or Somerset Singers,* ed. R. L. Tongue, Routledge, Kegan & Paul, London, 1968

Dorothy Neal Ballantyne for 'Carol for a New Zealand Child'

Big Sky Music for Bob Dylan 'Father of night' from *Writings and Drawings by Bob Dylan* © 1972 Bob Dylan, pub. Jonathan Cape, London, 1973

The Estate of the late Charles Brasch for 'I read your signature' from his *Collected Poems,* ed. Alan Roddick, Oxford University Press, Auckland, 1984

The Estate of the late Helen Diana Clyde for 'Children's Christmas Hymn'

Columbia University Press for Paul Engle 'Lord of each soul' from *American Hymns Old and New,* ed. A. Christ-Janer, C. W. Hughes and C. S. Smith, Columbia University Press, New York, 1980

Wm. B. Erdmans for John Bennett, 'Pentecost'

David Higham Associates for Charles Causley, 'Three masts has the thrusting ship' and 'I am the great sun' from his *Collected Poems 1951–1975,* Macmillan Ltd., London, 1983

Hope Publishing Co. for Jaroslav Vajda, 'Now the silence', © 1969 Hope Publishing Co., Carol Stream, Il 60186

Faber and Faber for Anne Ridler 'Young beam of heaven' from *A Matter of Life and Death,* Faber and Faber, London, 1959

Faber and Faber for Richard Wilbur 'A stable lamp is lighted' from *Advice to a Prophet and Other Poems,* Faber and Faber, 1953

The Hymn Society of America for Frank von Christenson 'Eternal Spirit of the Living Christ'

The Joint Board of Christian Education for Roland Giese 'The helper', 'Father forgive' and Start again'

The Estate of the late Alice Meynell for 'Unto us a Son is given'

Shirley Murray for 'A New Zealand Carol' and 'Carol'

Alphabetical index of hymns

A New Zealand carol	40
A song of Abraham	46
A song of David	47
A stable lamp is lighted	38
A summer carol	17
All we asked you gave and more	4
Ballad of the fishermen	14
But I say unto you	11
Caring	55
Carol	44
Carol for a New Zealand child	41
Carol of cold comfort	18
Children's Christmas hymn	42
Christ the cornerstone	23
Christ our joy	21
Christ joyful	13
Eternal Spirit of the living Christ	34
Father forgive	53
Father of night	30
For the gift of laughter	5
Godpoint	25
Great ring of light	7
He came singing love	1
How much am I worth?	54
I am the great sun	31
I've never seen an elephant	56
I read your signature	45
If all my youthful strength	15
In this familiar place	2
Jesus thy boundless love	33
Lord of all love	16
Lord of each soul	27
Matthew was a lonely man	12
My Father's ground	10
Now the silence	28
Out of such sun and air	24

Pentecost   32
Prayer of protection   35
Psalm 90   8
Psalm 151   52
Put me down for a victory crown   57
Seek and you shall find   49
Sing, sing, and what shall we sing?   50
Son of the carpenter   26
Song of the wilderness   6
Start again   29
The coming of Christ   22
The first night   43
The four evangelists   48
The helper   51
The mighty sun   20
Three masts has the thrusting ship   39
Unto us a Son is given   37
Voices   9
When Joseph and Mary were turned from the inn   19
Where the road runs out   3
Young beam of heaven   36